BOXES
BASKETS
& POTS

SANDRA FORTY

CW00326427

SANDRA FORTY

BOXES BASKETS & POTS

LifeStyle

Photography © Collins and Brown

Publisher: Lisa Simpson
Designer: Emily Cook
Picture researcher: Sarah Epton

This edition first published in Great Britain in 2000 by
LifeStyle
An imprint of Parkgate Books
London House, Great Eastern Wharf, Parkgate Road,
London SW11 4NQ

© Parkgate Books
A Division of Collins and Brown

A CIP catalogue record for this book is available from
the British Library.

ISBN 1-902617-05-3

PRINTED AND BOUND IN CHINA

INTRODUCTION

Container gardening has seen a tremendous increase in popularity in recent years as part of a general renewal of interest in plants and flowers and as an essential element in improving the quality of life.

Right: Citrus trees, such as this lemon, make easily grown and attractive container plants, especially when in fruit. However, all citrus have quite nasty thorns and will need protection from frost and cold winds over winter.

Far Right: Petunias, fuchsias and geraniums are some of the most reliable plants for windowboxes and hanging baskets. With regular watering, feeding and dead-heading they will flower happily until mid-autumn at least.

MUCH of this is down to the influence of television and magazines; with greater leisure time on our hands, a (potentially) labour-intensive pastime like gardening can be given more attention. A word of warning though for the uninitiated — gardening is hugely addictive: the more you do the more you will want to do. Luckily, as hobbies go it is one of the more economic (compare it to regular theatre going, following a football team or a golf habit).

Furthermore you don't even have to leave home for the most part unless you want to. This is where container gardening really comes into its own — many a potential gardener lives in a flat or somewhere there is no obvious available space within which to grow plants. However, containers can be used in the smallest spaces — window ledges, balconies, up the side of a staircase or simply as hanging baskets which can project out over otherwise unusable areas.

In addition our towns, villages and cities have noticeably become more colourful and eco-friendly over recent years with local authorities planting up cheerful hanging baskets in shopping areas, as well as taking

INFORMATIVE & INSPIRATIONAL **IDEAS** FOR CONTAINER GARDENING

Above: Container gardening is becoming more popular every year as new gardeners' discover that you don't have to have a conventional garden to enjoy the delights and satisfaction of growing plants.

INFORMATIVE &
INSPIRATIONAL
IDEAS FOR
CONTAINER
GARDENING

more care of municipal park areas. On an individual scale, too, far more people are putting attractive windowboxes on their homes and growing plants in pots around their patio areas. Come springtime, garden centres and greengrocers explode under the weight of bedding plants and plants for hanging baskets and containers.

A further advantage of growing plants in containers is that if your garden soil is poor or inaccessible under, say, a large pan of concrete, you can still grow plants and give them an excellent growing medium into the bargain. Container gardening is ideal for small town gardens where the patio is entirely covered in concrete. A lush, even tropical, effect can be created by installing one big feature — a large pot, a fountain or perhaps a statue — then filling much of the remainder of the space with big dramatic foliage plants such as bamboo, *Fatsia japonica*, camellia and phormiums, infilling with flowering seasonal plants in smaller containers for spot colour. In a limited area an effective trick is to use collections of the same plant in the same colour or colour range for massed impact.

It is amazing how a different look can be achieved by changing the details of a scheme around a base framework which essentially remains the same year to year. The beauty of growing plants in pots, of course, is

that you can change your colour scheme year to year if you want: completely white one year, a riot of every possible colour the next and then, perhaps, more refined golds and blues the following, and so on.

Your container garden should be considered as a whole; not just the plants or only the containers — you must see how they work together and how they fit into their situation. The rest is up to you, the style you want to achieve, the look — perhaps brightening up an otherwise dull corner, framing a doorway or filling a patio with colour and foliage.

When you view the project as a whole, first of all decide what kind of effect you want — classical and formal or informal and unfussy; this decision will include shape and, to some extent, colour. The other major factors are the containers themselves. They don't have to match or be of the same material by any means, but the result will be more effective if they have a cohesion of size, colour or shape. The 'bones' of your container garden will be made up of the containers themselves, perhaps with one especially striking feature such as a statue or particularly striking pot and a few evergreen perennials which will give your garden interest and form even in the dark days of winter when nothing much is happening.

Always check over a plant before buying it; look for healthy leaves and

Left: These white-themed plants are being used to brighten what could otherwise be a dull corner of a small town garden. The *Lilium longiflorum*, although only lasting in flower for a few weeks, will fill the air with heavenly scent.

Below: A large terracotta planter filled to the brim with flowers and foliage makes an ideal focal point. Height is provided by *Melianthus major* and artemisia. White daisy-like osteospermums, trailing blue *Malva sylvestris* 'Primley Blue' and marguerites fill in.

Above: A simple planting of two or three single-colour petunias makes a bright spot of colour. The plants will trail attractively as they grow through the summer.

Right: A hanging basket is usually seen from a low vantage position so it is important that trailing plants are used. Here a white busy lizzie is teamed with trailing plants such as begonia, blue lobelia and _Helichrysum petiolare_.

INFORMATIVE &
INSPIRATIONAL
IDEAS FOR
CONTAINER
GARDENING

strong shoots with plenty of buds to come. Avoid sickly looking plants, ones with damaged leaves and anything that has been attacked by pests — especially if it/they are still lurking on the plant. The chances are that when you buy a plant it will come in a plastic container and, furthermore, if it is a houseplant it will be in a soilless peat-based compost. This is entirely for reasons of weight for the grower and retailer rather than for the good of the plant — because this makes the plant very light and therefore cheaper to transport. Such plants dry out very quickly and need careful looking after.

Something to consider before any real trouble occurs is whether you want to be organic in approach or use chemicals to keep problems at bay. Hand removal of pests is organic as is trapping; on the other hand, spraying (unless with a soap solution) is non-organic. By encouraging birds and beneficial insects like ladybirds into your garden, nature will take care of many, but not all, pests.

Otherwise, organic control of pests is by way of using natural predators which parasitize the offending pests. The disadvantage of this approach is that you need a population of the invader (the host) before the parasites can get to work. By extrapolation, the parasites dies off when the hosts disappear and a reapplication of parasites is necessary next time an infestation occurs.

TOP10

container plants

These are the ten indispensable container plants — as good as guaranteed to give a successful display of colour and growth even for the novice gardener. However, only ivy is hardy enough to withstand a winter outdoors, although all of them can come successfully through a mild winter given a sheltered position.

Top and above: The only real drawback of the popular daisy-like flowers of osteospermum are their relatively limited colour range.

Bottom: Pelargoniums (commonly called geraniums) are probably the most easily grown container plants.

Opposite page, top: Busy lizzies are useful for growing in a shady spot where they will flower happily regardless of how much sunshine they get.

Opposite page, bottom: Conversely petunias need sunshine for successful flowering.

01	Busy lizzie	**06**	Lobelia
02	Ivy	**07**	Polyanthus
03	Petunia	**08**	Geranium/pelargonium
04	Tuberous begonia	**09**	Helychrysum
05	Osteospermum	**10**	Fuchsia

INFORMATIVE &
INSPIRATIONAL
IDEAS FOR
CONTAINER
GARDENING

TOP10 foliage plants

All these plants are evergreen and, with the exception of ferns, will provide a year-round display of foliage — so they can provide the 'structure' of a patio or container display.

Above: Trailing *Helichrysum petiolare* is an invaluable 'filler' as well as being attractive in its own right.

Right: Hebes are grown for their evergreen foliage and make good all-year round container plants. Additionally, they have the bonus of flowering with either purple, blue, pink or white flower spikes.

01	Ivy
02	Ballotta
03	Box (*Buxus*)
04	Ferns
05	Bamboo
06	Helichrysum
07	*Acuba japonica*
08	Hebe
09	*Fatsia japonica*
10	Phormium

INFORMATIVE &
INSPIRATIONAL
IDEAS FOR
CONTAINER
GARDENING

TOP10 climbing plants

Too many people forget the vertical dimension when it comes to container gardening. With these plants your container display will fill out and assume a maturity which could otherwise be lacking. All except ivies flower, and all except ivies and evergreen honeysuckles are deciduous, so they will lose their leaves in winter.

01	Passion flower
02	*Cobaea scandens*
03	Morning Glory/Convolvulus
04	Climbing rose
05	Clematis
06	Canary creeper/ *Tropeoleum canariensis*
07	Honeysuckle/Lonicera
08	*Solanum jasminiodes*
09	Ivy
10	Climbing hydrangea

Above: *Lonicera periclymenum* 'Belgica'. Honeysuckles tend to perform best in shade and not all are perfumed: check the label or ask the grower about preferred growing positions and fragrance.

Left: Climbing roses make a most romantic backdrop. Choose varieties that are not too vigorous or thorny. Also check the length of their flowering season — some flower in a single 'flush', when they look absolutely breathtaking but only for two or three weeks. Additionally, Not all varieties are scented.

TOP 10

large plants

For impact even only one or two large plants will make a significant difference on a patio. Left to grow in a garden all these plants will grow large in time; within the confines of a container they will be smaller than this but still larger than average. They must, however, be well fed and watered, and pruned, when necessary, to contain their growth. Canna, agave and oleander will need protection from winter frosts as will some of the more tender bamboos. However, the shelter of a wall, especially in a city microclimate, will help them to survive the winter.

01	Hydrangea
02	Rhododendron
03	Bamboo
04	*Fatsia japonica*
05	Camellia
06	Yucca
07	*Canna indica*
08	*Nerium oleander*
09	*Agave americana*
10	*Zantedeschia aethiopica*

Above: Mop-head hydrangeas have long-lasting 'flowers' (properly called bracts) that will last through the winter if dried.

Right: Pink *Camellia x williamsii* flowers in spring provided the frost does not ruin the blooms.

Far right: A sophisticated white and blue scheme from hydrangeas, nicotiana, lobelia and *Convolvulus sabatius*.

INFORMATIVE &
INSPIRATIONAL
IDEAS FOR
CONTAINER
GARDENING

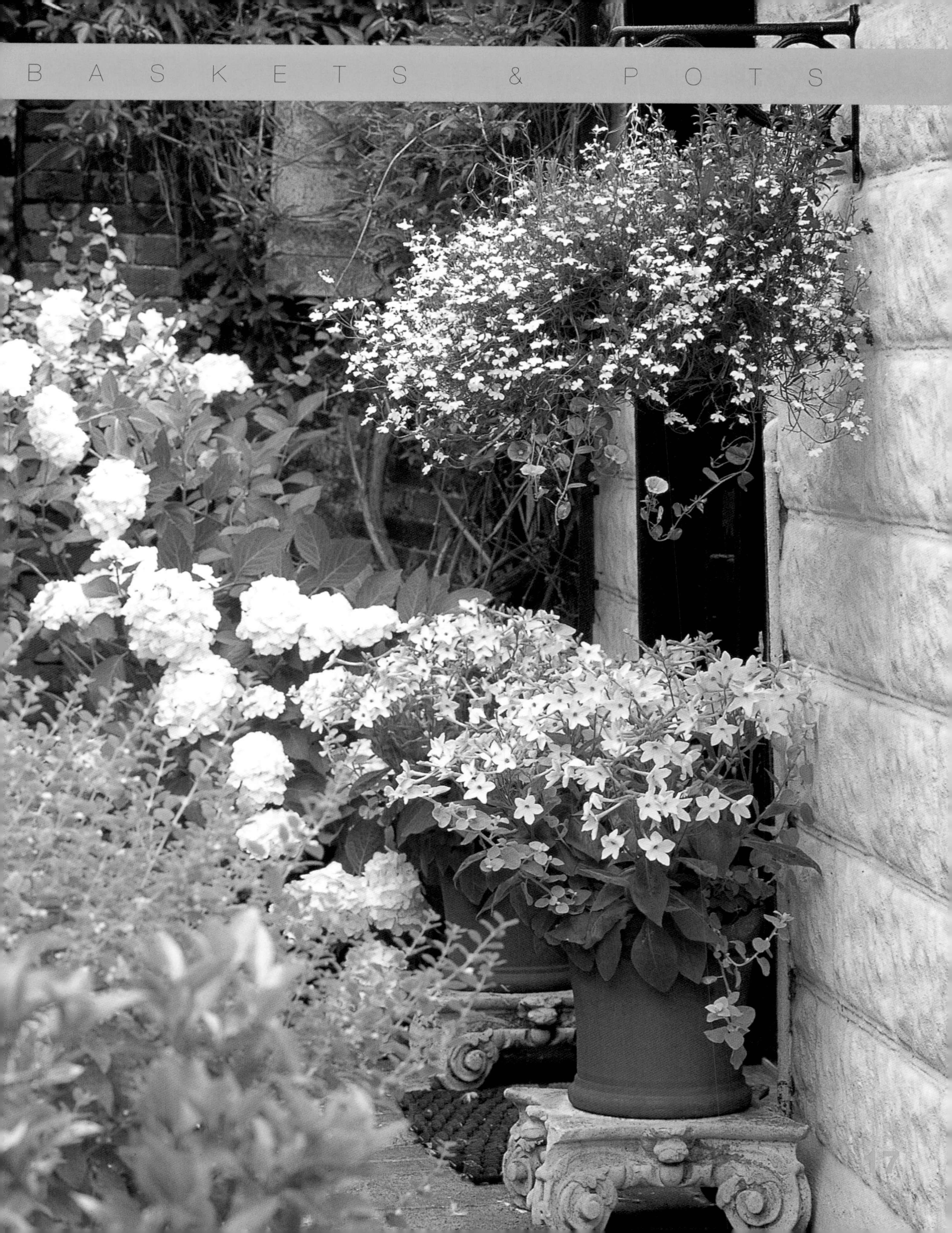

POTS ALL YEAR ROUND

One of the very nicest things about growing plants in containers is that they can vary with the seasons: with a bit of forethought a container garden can have something of interest looking spectacular at every time of year. Of course winter is the hardest time of year to achieve a lot of colour, but by using evergreens as a framework, splashes of colour from plants such as winter pansies and polyanthus can be used as highlights.

Here is a photographic guide to different seasonal plant arrangements, showing how the container can vary with the seasons.

Right: A small terracotta windowbox can give early spring cheer with a selection of pink, red and white flowers. The tallest are pink *Primula obconica* and *P. malacoides*. In the centre, red cineraria (though this is frost-tender), is flanked by red primula and white *Anemone blanda*; fine-leaved ivy is used as a filler.

INFORMATIVE & INSPIRATIONAL **IDEAS** FOR CONTAINER GARDENING

Above: Although rather tender, this dwarf *Clematis cartmanii* will flower in late spring. Other spring clematis are hardier and among the earliest flowering climbers. For containers, avoid the most vigorous varieties.

Left: Even a simple arrangement of crocus bulbs such as these can make a cheerful contribution to spring days. Remember that crocus flowers open out in the sunshine but remain shut in the shade.

Spring

Right: Summer is the easiest time to arrange a varied and interesting plant scheme. Here, pots of white marguerites, blue lobelia and silver-leaved cineraria liven up some garden steps.

INFORMATIVE &
INSPIRATIONAL
IDEAS FOR
CONTAINER
GARDENING

Summer

Another simple but effective use of a terracotta windowbox. The background is an Angel geranium, in front of which is the pink-leaf spotted *Hypoestes phyllostachya, Verbena x hybrida* and, right at the front, trailing ivy and clover-leafed *Oxalis articulata*.

Autumn

For late autumn/early winter plantings it is a nice idea to keep the plants themselves bright — hence the extensive use of variegated plants here. A striped *Cordyline australis* spreads dramatically out of the centre, complimented by white ornamental cabbage and variegated ivy.

Winter

Winter planting is inevitably much more limited, but low growing heathers and colourful primroses and polyanthus make a pretty grouping.

Year round pots

Right: There are many plants that look good all year round and many of them are primarily foliage plants. These ground-hugging succulent houseleeks (*Sempervivum* sp.) need gritty soil and sunshine. Mature plants flower after two or three years then die, but leave behind small offsets which can be replanted.

INFORMATIVE &
INSPIRATIONAL
IDEAS FOR
CONTAINER
GARDENING

Foliage

Left: Trailing plants can be planted together to make the most of their different leaf shape and colour. Here a mixture of tradescantia, ivy, asparagus fern, *Cissus antarctica* and *Saxifraga stolonifera*.

Below: There are many different shade-loving plants which make unusual and attractive groupings. This selection shows a fern underplanted with *Alchemilla mollis* and a fine leaf ivy.

Shade

CONTAINERS

For most gardeners the type of container used is a matter of taste and preference. Cost, of course, comes into it but so does the effect you are aiming for — sophisticated, formal, informal, classic, modern or any other style. The siting of your containers is also of primary importance.

There are many different shapes, sizes and materials for pots and containers — plastic (ideal for roof gardens), terracotta, stone, pottery, etc.

Right: Reconstituted stone containers are easily bought in a wide variety of shapes, sizes and styles.

Far right: Tall containers don't necessarily need tall plants. Here low growing *Lysimachia nummularia* 'Aurea' — although not the obvious choice — actually makes a very effective planting.

MANY of the urns and ornamental containers we see around the shops and garden centres are made of cement or reconstituted stone. These are made in moulds and so are available in quantity and in a huge variety of shapes and styles. Good quality containers last indefinitely, although the more poorly made ones — usually but not always the cheaper ones — tend to start crumbling around the edges after a few winter seasons. Little maintenance other than a light scrubbing to remove mud is necessary for these containers.

They are good for permanent plantings as they are heavy and durable — two prime qualities necessary for permanence. Also, in common with all large containers, it is best to place the pot on terracotta or ceramic feet to lift the base clear of the ground and allow free drainage away from the base.

INFORMATIVE & INSPIRATIONAL IDEAS FOR CONTAINER GARDENING

Cement/reconstituted stone

Terracotta

THE conventional flowerpot that everyone thinks of is an ordinary clay pot. It comes in a range of sizes from the smallest thumb pot to enormous, and consequently is everything from very cheap to very expensive. Unless specified, it will not be frost-proof: acceptable for ordinary pots, but not if you have spent a great deal of money. Some pots are elaborately moulded with intricate decorations; if you have one of these and you think that it is not frost-proof, take it into shelter during the winter so that it won't be in danger of cracking in frosts and snow.

The more expensive terracotta pots will be frost proof and can be left safely outside during the winter. It is always worth checking before you buy whether or not a pot is frost proof — there will usually be some indication. Generally speaking, pots made in hot countries like Greece or Spain will not be frost proof.

Terracotta is aesthetically pleasing and easily fits in with most schemes — especially when the pot has aged and lost its bright new colour which can be alarmingly orange with some clays. It is, however, fragile and will shatter instantly if it sustains anything more than a light knock. The good news is that the resultant pot shards can be used as crocks in the bottom of the next container you plant up. Terracotta can also be painted to fit a particular colour scheme.

Clay pots dry out quickly and so plants in them need frequent watering in warm weather as the porous terracotta will 'pull' any moisture into itself and quickly dry out the compost inside. Conversely, terracotta pots will get covered in green slime (algal growth) very quickly if they are kept in damp conditions with saturated compost.

Weight can be a problem with terracotta: pots full of soil-based compost will be quite heavy, while a large pot will be impossible to move without assistance. This is a point to remember when placing a large pot as a feature or otherwise — it will be difficult to move elsewhere should you change your mind about its position.

When reusing a clay pot it is necessary to scrub away accumulated dirt and any lurking pests and diseases before committing the life of a new plant to it. Then the pot should be soaked before replanting so that it does not extract all the moisture from the compost leaving little or none for the plant inside.

Chimney pots make attractive containers and add height to a collection of pots — useful to fill visual space in a plant arrangement. They are heavy but surprisingly brittle and need careful placing before being filled with plants as they become very difficult to move once full. The entire length of the pot does not need to be filled with compost: other material such as rubble, ordinary garden soil (actually not so ideal as it comes with its full accompaniment of pests and soil-borne diseases) or polystyrene pieces can fill the majority of the length. Use a block of polystyrene, plastic or even wood to block off the bottom and either fill the top with compost and plant up, or just put a plant already in a plastic container in the top. The advantage of this is that when the plant has stopped looking its best — stopped flowering or perhaps succumbed to growth problems — the entire pot can be taken out and replaced.

Some terracotta containers are partially glazed: these retain water better but do not always have a drainage hole and can become waterlogged. Use them as sleeves or cache pots for a smaller, less attractive, pots.

Plastic

THIS is the cheapest type of container, the lightest as well as the most versatile. Today enterprising manufacturers produce plastic containers that can pass for terracotta, lead, wood or marble. The best are convincing — and quite expensive, but still only a fraction of the cost of the real thing.

Plastic containers are ideal for use on roof gardens or windowledges, but make sure they are secured or weighted down or they will blow over or even sailing away altogether!

Plastic pots are increasingly available in a range of colours, so they can be easily and economically used to accentuate any colour theme that you might choose for your garden. Most plastic is durable, but after a few seasons becomes brittle from the effects of ultraviolet; the only exception to this is the more flexible black polypropylene container.

Plastic is the complete opposite of clay when it comes to water retention in the compost. Plastic extracts no moisture from its surroundings; it is impermeable, so a plant needs less watering in a plastic pot than in clay.

Furthermore, being impervious to moisture, plant roots are kept a little warmer in winter than those in china or clay containers.

Because of its impermeability, it is easier to overwater a plant in a plastic container; but the water retention can be put to good use in places where drought can be a problem or if you're going away on holiday. This does not mean that plastic containers will not dry out; they do, but just take longer.

Wood

WOODEN troughs and half barrels are the most frequently used wooden containers. Timber rots over a period of time, so to maintain a wooden container a wood preservative must be applied every couple of years if the container is to have any durability. Also, it helps if the container is raised slightly off the ground so that water can run off and away rather than being trapped by the lip so that it ends up sitting in a puddle of water.

Timber is a good natural insulator and will provide plant roots a degree of protection against cold. But, once filled with compost a wooden container is heavy, especially the half barrels. So, in common with most large containers,

consider carefully the position before filling one.

Wood is the easiest material to use if you want to make your own containers: it can be cut to any size to fit a particular location — especially

useful for windowboxes. Use pressure-treated wood or a hardwood timber from a renewable source rather than a softwood such as pine, which will rot very quickly.

The most formal wooden containers

are the attractive Versailles tubs; these four-square containers sit off the ground on small feet and have a spherical finial at each of the corners. They are usually painted white and are seen to best effect with clipped bays or box.

Hanging baskets

IN recent years more and more people are using hanging baskets to decorate the outside of their homes. Almost all are made of plastic-coated wire coloured green, black or white; less frequently they are made from galvanised metal. Baskets can vary in size from 10 inches in diameter to about 25 inches. Alternatively, some hanging baskets are no more than plastic flower pots with attached plastic arms that culminate in a hook. They have an attached drip tray to prevent the water shooting straight through the compost. These containers usually arrive with the plant or plants in situ: all you need to do is hang them up.

Wire baskets require a lining to hold the compost in position. You can find liners ready made to size and shape in a variety of plastics, a biodegradable cardboard-like bowl made from peat, or matting made from coir. The traditional method is to use fresh sphagnum moss which will continue growing until it forms into a mat around the plant roots. This natural resource is increasingly hard to find; indeed, many gardeners consider its use unethical as this depletes stocks from the wild.

INFORMATIVE & INSPIRATIONAL **IDEAS** FOR CONTAINER GARDENING

China/pottery

GLAZED pottery containers are readily available in shops and garden centres across the country. They come in a marvellous range of colours and sizes and can be used to great effect for dramatic arrangements of pots and plants. They have similar advantages and disadvantages as terracotta — breakability, weight, expense, durability — but are more weather proof, particularly to frosts. than terracotta. A few years ago it was difficult to find a large glazed container under £40 or £50; now a flood of Far Eastern imports has seen prices come down considerably and they are much more affordable.

Left: A glazed pot can be used as a mini water garden provided that there is no drainage hole in the base.

Right: A large stone trough makes a magnificent garden feature and can be interestingly filled with a wide variety of plants.

INFORMATIVE &
INSPIRATIONAL
IDEAS FOR
CONTAINER
GARDENING

Stone

TRADITIONALLY used outside cottages for alpines, old stone troughs rescued from farmyards are eagerly sought by gardeners as they are among the most attractive containers for a patio garden. Frequently made from a hard stone such as granite, they require mechanical assistance to move into position and a small fortune to buy. Ideally they need a drainage hole in the bottom to allow excess water to escape (an old stone sink will already have one); but if this proves impossible to achieve, a very thick layer of crocks or rubble must be laid along the bottom of the trough or your plants will simply drown during wet weather. One alternative to this is to use the stone trough as a mini pool and grow aquatic plants instead.

By using containers made of local stone your plantings will blend into their surrounds in a naturalistic way. Furthermore, within quite a short period of time, a stone container will start to weather attractively and, depending on its position, grow moss or lichen on its outer surfaces.

Marble, of course, comes into the stone category and is generally only found in the very best quality containers carved into elaborate urns. While marble weathers well, white marble will quickly discolour and is surprisingly brittle, so it needs to be placed where the container is in little danger of suffering inadvertent knocks.

Fibreglass & novelty

INCREASINGLY used for more elaborate imitation containers, fibreglass has two great advantages: it is light and it is remarkably durable. These assets make it ideal for rooftop gardens where weight is a consideration. On top of this, fibreglass won't be damaged by frost or water and is impermeable to water, so the only evaporation is through the open top of the container. It does, however, in time become brittle from exposure to ultraviolet light unless treated with a suitable surface sealant.

Almost anything that can hold soil can be used as a plant container; in the right place and with clever planting many can look effective. However, an odd assortment of peculiar containers easily looks messy and misses the point entirely.

INFORMATIVE & INSPIRATIONAL **IDEAS** FOR CONTAINER GARDENING

Lead planters

ANOTHER extremely heavy container, lead planters were often the old water butts from grand houses. Now being made commercially again specifically for gardeners, they are heavy and expensive but magnificent in the right setting. Remember, however, that lead is highly toxic, so do not use it in any position where an animal might lick it or a small child be tempted to handle it.

Far left: Even brightly painted tin cans can look stylish when used with wit and imagination.

Left: Lead planters are altogether grander containers and require equally imposing planting. Once *in situ* they are next to impossible to move as they are so heavy.

Metal

OLD water tanks can be used as containers for plants, but as they tend to be on the large side it is perhaps best to use them for aquatic plants rather than attempt to fill them with suitable soil. Metal corrodes and so any such container will need to be treated with a rust killer.

Galvanised metal containers are now available for plants and can look very effective, especially for a contemporary setting. The galvanising of iron leaves the object a bright shiny silver, but this rapidly tarnishes to a dull lead grey and goes very well with green foliage.

Occasionally old copper boilers are used as effective plant containers. Originally bright and shiny, copper ages to an attractive verdigris colour which blends well with most plants. Remember that copper is an excellent conductor of heat, so avoid tender plants which would suffer unnecessarily in cold weather.

**Above and right:
Ordinary galvanised metal
containers can be jazzed
up with simple decorative
patterns. In these
examples the silvery metal
catches the sunlight while
the gold metallic paint
adds extra glitter.**

INFORMATIVE &
INSPIRATIONAL
IDEAS FOR
CONTAINER
GARDENING

PLANTING A CONTAINER

Having acquired a container and decided upon its contents the next thing to do is plant it up.

DEPENDING on the type of plant you've chosen, you need good compost — garden soil is not suitable for container-grown plants because it already contains pests and diseases, may well be poor anyway and will not contain sufficient if any natural fertilizer. You need to buy enough sterilised compost for your pots. Container-grown plants need special care as their roots cannot search beyond the container for extra nutrition and water — that is your responsibility as the gardener.

The choice of growing medium depends on what type of plants you want to grow and how long you expect them to last. In other words a soil-based compost is essential for a long-term plant, but for something which is only going to last a season this is less important. Generally speaking, a multi-purpose compost is best for most plants. Containing grit, gravel and slow-release fertilizer, it is light, clean and sterile but will dry out quickly. Made from peat (or peat substitutes such as vermiculite, mica, cocoa shells, coir or shredded bark), plus base fertilizer and coarse grit. Furthermore, you can get pre-treated compost as protection against certain pests such as the increasingly prevalent vine weevil. For long-term plants which will stay in

position for the foreseeable future use a mixture such as John Innes No 3. This contains a scientifically measured amount of fertilizer, trace elements and soil which will feed, nourish and support your plants. For bulbs like hyacinths and narcissus use specially prepared bulb fibre.

If you are planting a roof garden, weight of soil becomes a prime consideration and you should look into some of the lighter mixtures. One excellent way of reducing the weight of a fully planted pot is to fill the bottom third to half with polystyrene pieces. This inert substance provides bulk without weight and has the added bonus of providing a measure of insulation to the plant roots, something that is very useful for containers in an exposed situation such as a rooftop. However, in such situations the containers need to be anchored firmly.

The first thing to check is that the container is clean and that it has one or more drainage holes. This is important as water must be able to escape otherwise the soil will become waterlogged and the plants will die. May pots come with a marked drainage hole which has not actually been breached (to give the purchaser the option if, perhaps, you are just going to use the container as an outer 'envelope'

INFORMATIVE &
INSPIRATIONAL
IDEAS FOR
CONTAINER
GARDENING

01 Take a clean terracotta pot with sufficient drainage holes. Place pot shards or large stones over the hole itself and add a layer of shingle or pebbles for extra drainage.

02 Half fill the pot with suitable compost and add some slow-release fertilizer across the surface. This will feed the plant when the temperature gets warm enough but remain inactive during cold weather.

03 At this stage some water-retaining granules can be prepared. These will reduce the need for frequent watering during hot weather and will extend the period between waterings. Follow the instructions on the packet to inflate the granules.

(continued on page 41)

and you don't want the water flooding too far.). With plastic the hole can often just be punched out. Clay and fibreglass are more problematic and the only answer is to drill a hole. Don't, whatever you do, try to open the hole in a terracotta pot with a hammer and nail — that'll only shatter the container. Find some masking tape (ideally) or similar, and make an X across the intended hole with the tape. Then, very carefully but firmly, use a drill to open the hole. The tape should prevent the container from fracturing and breaking.

Depending on the size of the container, more than one hole will be needed: it is better to have too many than too few but don't make so many that all the soil washes out the first time you water! Be guided by your other pots. Then, to stop the compost washing away, put a few crocks (broken bits of pot) or stones over the hole before partially filling the container with compost — fill the container to where the plant's lowest roots currently reach. Measure this by sitting the plant — still in the pot it was bought in — on the compost in the new, half-filled, pot. Keep adding soil to the container until the plant will sit comfortably when all the rest is filled up, leaving a good inch clear of soil to the rim. Then take the plant out of its pot, gently tease out the roots to encourage them to explore beyond their existing pot size and carefully infill around the plant with soil. Alternatively, fill the

container with compost to the required depth, until an inch or so below the rim, then dig out a suitably sized hole for the plant.

Decide how you want your plants arranged within the container, then carefully put them in. If the plants are in dry compost, put the entire pot up to the soil level into a bucket of water. If the plants are in soilless compost you can tell whether they are dry by their lack of weight and the shrinkage of compost from around the pot sides. A dry pot will also float when put into the water. Wait until the pot sinks to indicate that the soil has resaturated before planting up — this can sometimes take up to 20 minutes. If you pot a plant with such desiccated compost the roots will be strangled and dry and are unlikely to get sufficient water to recover. When finished, gently but firmly compact the compost around the roots and stems to secure the plants. Then give the entire container a thorough watering. Don't be surprised when this first deluge washes some compost out from the drainage hole — it's inevitable.

At this stage, you can add a slow-release fertilizer to the compost if you wish. When the weather is warm enough, slow-release fertilizers introduce fertilizer into the compost when the plants are watered. This saves you having to keep to a feeding routine but doesn't let you adjust the type and balance of the plant food according to season and need.

INFORMATIVE & INSPIRATIONAL **IDEAS** FOR CONTAINER GARDENING

(continued from page 39)

04 When they are ready the granules can be mixed into the compost distributing them as evenly as possible. Granules are especially useful for thirsty plants, hanging baskets and plants that will receive infrequent watering.

05 The largest plant is placed in position first. Tease out the roots a little to encourage them to grow outwards and make sure that the top of the rootball will rest a couple of inches below the rim of the pot.

06 Decide how you want to arrange the plants and then add them, filling and firming in the compost as you go. Finally water the plants in well so that they get off to a good start.

STEP-BY-STEP

Planting up a small trough or shallow container

AS troughs of this type tend to be recycled containers, first of all make sure that it is clean and free from any old compost or soil. Any lingering dirt could harbour pests and diseases. Secondly, check for a good drainage hole — such a shallow container will require an outlet or the plant roots will rot in the water which will pool at the base of the trough. (For a deep trough this is not such a problem — a good deep layer of drainage crocks can keep roots clear of the water level and reduce the risk of rot.)

A small trough such as this is ideal for alpine plants — in this case, sedums, dianthus (better known as pinks), and sempervivums (houseleeks). Houseleeks are traditionally believed to keep lightning away and so were planted on rooftops in the old days.

01 Cover the drainage hole with a crock (broken piece of pot or stone) and then fill about one third of the depth of the container with a mixture of 50:50 compost and coarse sand or fine gravel. Even out the level and gently firm in place.

02 To get the composition right you may find it helpful to position the plants (while still in their pots) on the compost so you can arrange their colouring and heights. Having decided your layout, take the plants out of their containers one at a time. Carefully tease out the roots trying not to break them. Begin to fill in the compost.

03 As you continue to add plants fill in the gaps with compost. As we are planting alpines, scatter some more sand or gravel around the base of each plant to encourage drainage. Alpines hate to sit in a puddle of water as their crowns easily rot in such conditions.

04 After completing planting, even out the surface compost and gently firm each plant in position. Scatter a little more gravel over the surface and then water the plants in gently, so as not to wash away the surface compost.

PLANTS USED
Sedum spathulifolium **'Purpureum'**
Sedum s. **'Capo Blanco'**
Sempervivum **'Alpha'**

INFORMATIVE &
INSPIRATIONAL
IDEAS FOR
CONTAINER
GARDENING

Planting a container with bulbs

MANY bulbs make good container plants and some of the best — certainly most appreciated — are those that flower early in the year before there is much else activity in the garden. Bulbs such as crocus, daffodil, narcissus and hyacinth all make colourful spring companions. With just the minimum of care they are easy to grow, are guaranteed to flower, and can be discarded or planted into the border for the following years. Sadly they never 'do' as well in a pot in successive years. Spring bulbs should be planted about six months before flowering, and summer bulbs about three months before flowering.

01 Cover the drainage hole with a layer of crocks first to ensure good drainage. Spring bulbs do not require soil-based compost and are usually planted in a 50:50 mixture of bulb fibre and aggregate, in this case vermiculite. Bulbs should be planted to three times their diameter in depth under compost. Place them on the compost so that the root side faces down and the shoots face up — this is straightforward with bulbs but can be debatable with some

corms and tubers. If in doubt place the bulb on its side and let nature sort it out.

02 Fill the container with the rest of the compost and gently firm the surface to collapse any large air pockets around the bulbs.

03 Give the container a gentle watering sufficient to moisten the compost. Keep this up until the shoots break the surface, then water more freely. After flowering, cut off the dead heads but feed and care for the foliage until it dies down naturally if you want to keep the bulbs for another year (though not in the container). The bulbs can then be removed and planted out in the garden; they will not be as vigorous the second year but should recover for the third year.

STEP-BY-STEP

Planting a hanging basket

HANGING baskets are a very effective medium for displaying plants — as well as being a way of growing plants where no other method is possible. The real trick behind a successful hanging basket lies in the simple steps you take at planting time. Place trailing plants around the edges and lower down in the basket, keeping the upright growers for the top and centre.

01 Find a good size pot or bucket on which to stabilise the hanging basket while it is being worked on and planted. When not using a custom-made basket liner, use sphagnum moss (available in polythene bags at most garden centres in spring). Use it in thick wads to fill the lower hemisphere of the basket, within a few weeks it will grow over the wire frame of the basket.

02 Cut out a generous circle of black plastic and pierce it with drainage holes. Insert it into the basket over the layer of moss. Now make three or four slits in the plastic and carefully push the plant from the outside into the basket trying not to damage foliage or leaves — though they will quickly regrow.

03 When all three plants are inserted through the slits, fill the centre with potting mixture. Gently firm the plant roots and make sure they are properly covered with compost. At this stage you can, if you wish, add slow release fertilizer pellets and or water-retaining gel which will help to prevent the basket drying out too quickly.

04 Arrange and place the top plants into the basket. Firm them in and cover their roots with a good layer of compost. Don't fill the basket too full of compost or the water will just run straight off and not sink into the compost — this can become a problem in hot weather when the compost dries out and hardens. Check that the basket is nicely arranged with plants all around: a well planted basket will quickly fill out. Water the basket well and leave to drain before hanging in position.

INFORMATIVE &
INSPIRATIONAL
IDEAS FOR
CONTAINER
GARDENING

Planting a wall pot

SIMILAR rules apply for a wall pot
as for a hanging basket, except that
instead of being viewed from all
around, a wall pot will only show its
forward face.

PLANTS USED
Felicia capensis varigata
Scaevola
Glechoma hederacea
'Variegata'/Varigated ivy

01   This is a clay pot so it will
need a few drainage crocks in
the base. Fill the pot about a
third full with multi-purpose
compost.

02   Put the trailing plants on the
rim edge. Here a *Felicia
capensis* is being placed on the
right side of the pot. Make
sure the stems are able to trail
over the side. Spread the roots
out to balance the plant.

03   Add a little more compost
over the roots and add a
balancing second plant to the
other side of the container,
again making sure the trailing
stems hang over the side.

04   Place the variegated ground
ivy in the centre with the
more upright scavola behind,
to rest against the wall edge.
Fill the gaps with compost
to within a good inch of the
pot rim, firm all the plants
in carefully then water
them well.

STEP-BY-STEP

Using a wooden barrel

UNLIKE other containers, wooden barrels need attention before being used for planting, this goes for small as well as large barrels: the principle is the same. With a large barrel you will need to plant it in its growing position because the planted up barrel will be too heavy to move easily.

01 When you first get your barrel the chances are that the wood will have dried out and the joints will be open. To remedy this the wood needs a good soaking to allow the grain to swell up again.

02 If possible place the barrel on a large tray or container to prevent water seepage, then fill the barrel itself full of water. Afterwards, leave it for a few hours to allow the wood to swell and the joints to close up. When the barrel is intact again, throw away the excess water and allow the barrel to drain before you start planting.

03 Insert a large black plastic liner around the inside of the barrel, not forgetting to make a few drainage holes in the base of the liner. Do not tidy up the edge of the liner yet as the weight of the compost will pull the liner further into the barrel.

04 Depending on the root length of the plant, fill the bottom of the barrel about one third full of a good soil-based compost such as John Innes No 3. Knock the rose out of its pot and place it on the compost so that when the soil is added the base of the plant will lie about an inch below the rim. Fill up with compost and gently firm the rose in position, then trim off the surplus liner to compost level to make a neat finish. Move the barrel into its growing position before watering the plant — even a small barrel will become surprisingly heavy once it is watered.

PLANT USED
Rose

INFORMATIVE &
INSPIRATIONAL
I D E A S FOR
CONTAINER
GARDENING

Planting a large tree or shrub

WITH a permanent container plant such as a tree or shrub extra care needs to be taken to prepare exactly the right conditions for the plant. The container needs to be a good 5cm (2in) larger around the base of the rootball than its existing container. Also a tree will require a stake or stout cane to prevent it from being badly rocked in the wind.

01 Having found the right size container, fill the base with a good layer of crocks or pebbles. Using a good strong soil-based compost such as John Innes No 3, put a layer over the crocks judging so that when the plant is inserted the top of the rootball will lies about 2.5cm (1in) below the rim of the pot.

02 Carefully knock the plant — in this case an apple tree — from its container. You will need to support the weight with your hand under the rootball. Tease out the roots from the compact rootball to encourage the tree to send its roots sideways and not just round in circles as it has in the previous container. Spread the roots out and balance the tree in the centre of the pot.

03 As you fill the container, stand back to check that the tree is vertical and not leaning to one side. Gently compact the compost around the edges of the pot, then carefully insert a stake a good 5cm (2in) away from the stem, pushing it right to the base of the container. A little root damage is inevitable but should repair quickly. Loosely tie the plant to the support.

04 Fill the remainder of the pot with compost up to within 2.5cm (1in) of the rim, firming in gently as you go. Water the plant well by filling up to the rim. If necessary fill in with more compost if there is too much run-off. Keep the tree well watered particularly in summer and especially when in flower and fruit.

STEP-BY-STEP

Planting tall bulbs such as lilies

Lilies are among the loveliest of container plants but unfortunately they do not last more than about three weeks in flower. For this reason, plant up pots of lily bulbs at two or three week intervals so that you have a succession of lilies through summer. Many lilies have a powerful fragrance — especially at night — so place their containers near windows or seating areas where their scent can waft through the air.

MANY of the taller growing bulbs — such as lilies — need special care at planting time to ensure that their heavy flower heads don't flop too badly or overbalance the container. This staking is most easily done at planting time rather than later as the bulbs start growing when there is a danger of damaging the roots and bulbs as the stakes are being pushed in. Then, as the plants grow, carefully tie the stems to the stakes, being careful not to tie the twine so tight as to crush the stem.

01 For three lily bulbs select a good size clay pot, in this instance 35cm (14in) diameter. Cover the drainage hole with a good layer of crocks or pebbles. This has the dual advantage of weighting the pot and giving the compost the ability to drain freely, most important for lilies as their bulbs will rot if left in sodden compost for any length of time.

02 Using a good soil-based compost such as John Innes No 3, partially fill the pot so that when the lilies are planted the bulbs will be two and a half times their depth from the surface. Add a good layer of coarse sand or fine gravel — again to improve drainage — then space the bulbs out evenly. Fill the remainder of the pot with compost to 2.5cm (1in) or so below the rim of the pot.

03 Insert four or five canes 1.2m (4ft) long around the edge and push them to the base of the pot. (The length of the canes used should be 6–8in shorter than the final plant height.) Done at this stage there is no danger of damaging roots or bulbs. Leave the container to settle and don't water the lilies until their shoots start to pierce the surface of the compost.

04 As the lilies grow, carefully tie them in with garden twine every 15cm (6in). While doing this, arrange the stems so that they conceal as much of the stake as possible.

PLANT USED
Lilium 'Costa Blanca'

INFORMATIVE & INSPIRATIONAL **IDEAS** FOR CONTAINER GARDENING

05 When fully grown the foliage will conceal much of the staking and twine. Also it becomes obvious why it is so important to make the base of the container heavy enough to counteract the top heavy weight of the flowers.

PLANT GAZETTEER BY COLOUR

A number of plants come in variety of colours and combinations of colour; in the following listing they are entered in the colour category in which they predominate. For example, lobelia are usually blue, but also come in pink and white; while tulips and pansies, for example, are grown in the widest colour range possible. The gazetteer is by no means an exclusive list of plants which can be grown in containers, but rather a selective listing of some of the best, there are many, many more plants which will grow happily in containers

Furthermore, the plants are listed alphabetically by their common name (where they have a widely recognised one) followed by the correct Latin. Do try to learn the Latin names as you go along because this will help you find the exact plant you are looking for in the nursery or garden centre — whether you are in Britain, Australia, France, the United States or anywhere in the world — Latin names are universal, common names are local. Once you get interested and develop a feel for gardening, you'll be surprised how easy it is to pick up the proper names.

Right: A simple square container shows off these beautiful red and yellow tulips and orange pansies in full bloom.

INFORMATIVE & INSPIRATIONAL **IDEAS** FOR CONTAINER GARDENING

White

Bacopa/*Sutera cordata*
Perennial
Low growing plant ideal for spilling over the edges of a small container, windowbox or hanging basket, bacopa is usually grown as an annual although it will survive if given winter protection from the frosts. Give it a warm position and well drained multi compost. Feed and water every two weeks throughout the growing season.

Bitter Cress/*Cardamine trifolia*
Perennial
Flowering in spring bitter cress is an invasive plant which is best contained in a pot on its own. Give it moist multi-purpose compost and a sunny or semi-shade position. Once its flowering period is over it is unremarkable and is best removed.

Shasta Daisy/*Leucanthemum x superbum*
Hardy perennial
One of the traditional cottage garden flowers the large, daisy-like flowers which appear in mid to late summer enjoy plenty of sunshine and a well drained soil. If subjected to too much wind shasta daisies can flop over so they are best supported with stakes before they grow too tall (they get to about 3ft/1m high). After a season or two these hardy perennials will form a sizeable clump which will need splitting in four or five years.

Rock Rose/*Cistus*
Evergreen shrub
With attractive, fragile looking paper-like flowers cistus really enjoy a hot and sunny situation and will tolerate a degree of drying out. Most flowers only last a day but they are produced (depending on variety) throughout the summer in flushes. The flowers are usually white or shades of purple, mauve and pink. Cistus is one of the few plants which happily survives salt-laden air and so are commonly grown by the seaside. Give cistus free-draining soil and shelter from cold winter winds and snows — these Mediterranean plants will not survive a freezing cold winter. Lightly trim the plant only if necessary and do not disturb the roots once planted except to put into a larger container.

Angel's Trumpet/*Brugmansia*
Tender perennial
This South American small shrub is pollinated in nature by hummingbirds and is a truly exotic plant. It is also lethally poisonous — do not grow it anywhere near small children. However, it is lovely in a way no other plant manages; its long pendulous flowers — up to 6–10in (15–25cm) long (white, cream, yellow, pink or orange-red flushed) — only appear in a good sunny summer, but when they do they are a show stopper. Grow angel's trumpets in well drained John Innes

**Above: Common jasmine
(*Jasminium officinale*) is a
vigorous climber which
flowers in late summer/
early autumn. Its semi-
evergreen twining stems
will need cutting back
after flowering to control
the plant's size.**

**Right: Miniature
marguerites flower happily
all summer as long as the
dead flowers are snipped
off regularly. They also need
plenty of water and feeding.**

No 3 or a good light multi purpose
compost and place the container in
your sunniest spot but well out of
the wind. With time and shelter it
will grow to a good 6–8ft
(1.8–2.4m) even in a pot. Feed and
water well in the summer, much less
so when not actively growing. This
plant needs more than frost
protection in winter.

Jasmine
Climber

The common white *Jasmine
officinale* is a lovely heavily-scented
plant for a large container. It is a
vigorous climber and will need
to be grown against a fence or trellis
where it can twine its way
upwards, although it will still need
help with support by tying in the
long lax stems. Place it near a
window or eating area in a good
bright spot where its heady summer
fragrance can be enjoyed. Jasmine
loses its leaves in winter and can be
bitten back by the frost. Feed it
regularly in the growing season
and trim off long shoots to
encourage bushiness.

Winter Jasmine, *J.nudiflorum*,
has bright yellow flowers in the
winter months on bare but bright
green stems and provides a measure
of colour at a time when most plants
are dormant. The long lax stems
need tying to a support. After
flowering prune back the stems to
encourage bushy growth.

Lewisia
Perennial

Cheerful little plants flowering in a
range of bright colours the
'Cotyledon Hybrids' are good alpine
and windowbox plants. Give them a
semi-shade position in humus-rich
multi purpose compost. These small
(12in/30cm) evergreen perennials
form clumps of rosettes from which
they throw up stout stems with
multiple flower heads in early
summer. Of increasing interest to
plant breeders, these flowers also
come in the pink and purple range.

Lily
Bulb

There are many different types of
lily and they all make wonderful pot
plants. They are grown for their
magnificent flowers which sadly only
last for a matter of a few weeks, but
keep the plants, feed and water them
all summer and they'll flower again
the following years. Almost without
exception lilies need staking (see
page 48). Start them from bulbs
yourself or buy ready-grown plants.
Use them as 'spot' plants to
highlight a particular aspect — after
they have finished flowering move
them to a less prominent spot

Lilies are available in a
reasonably wide range of colours —
white, creams, reds, pinks, purples,
yellows and oranges. Many have a
wonderful heavy scent so place them
where this can be enjoyed; however,

be warned, the pollen on the end of the stamens can badly stain skin and clothes, if so much as touched — florists cut the pollen ends off open blooms for this reason.

Marguerite/*Chrysanthemum frutescens*
Hardy perennial
Enduringly popular, these large white daisy-like flowers appear throughout summer. Also confusingly known as *Argyranthemum frutescens*, the marguerite has made something of a comeback in recent years with the development and refinement of plants in a range of other colours which includes yellow and pink single and double forms. Valuable for continuous and prolific flowering throughout summer, they informally spill over the edges of their containers creating a most romantic, cottage garden-like effect.

They need plenty of room as they grow up to 3ft (1m) tall, give them plenty of sunshine, water and feed throughout the growing season. They need protection to survive the winter and will succumb to frosts.

Myrtle/*Myrtus communis*
Evergreen shrub
Redolent of the Mediterranean, the myrtle is a medium-sized aromatic bush which is covered in small white flowers in the summer. It relishes sitting in the full sun but will need

protection from cold wind and winter frost so it is best placed on a south or west facing wall out of the way of cold winds. Grow myrtle in fertile, well-drained soil and feed every two weeks in the growing season. Cutting back, or even just trimming the stems, encourages the plant to thicken up and grow more stems.

Narcissus
Bulb
Valuable for late winter and early

spring flowering, the narcissus is usually white, though it can also be yellow. It flowers for only a few short weeks after which you should cut off the dead heads. However, remember to feed and water the bulbs until the leaves die down. In common with other spring bulbs, they are unlikely to flower as successfully again unless planted out into the garden and even then it will take a couple of years before flowering resumes with any great strength.

Above: The hardy passion flower (*Passiflora caerulea*) is a useful screening plant. Its numerous tendrils will pull it up even the tallest wall.

Above right: *Rosa* 'Iceberg'. Roses are a must for many gardeners and there is a good choice of white varieties.

Right: Snowdrops are the heralds of spring and will grow well for one season in a small pot. Plant them after flowering into open ground where they will soon spread.

INFORMATIVE & INSPIRATIONAL **IDEAS** FOR CONTAINER GARDENING

Osteospermum
Half hardy perennial
In recent years these large daisy-like flowers have really taken off in popularity: their only drawback is their fairly limited colour range — white, cream, yellow, soft pink and purples. But once started they will bloom all summer for as long as the sunshine lasts provided the spent flower heads are cut off.

Passion flower/*Passiflora caerulea*
Climber
There are many different species of passion flower but only *P .caerulea* can survive freezing in winter. Despite this, the passion flower is one of the most distinctive, exotic-looking plants to grow, and after a hot summer mature plants will produce bright orange egg-sized fruits. It climbs vigorously by means of tendrils and will need a wall or somesuch to grow up. This passion flower loses the majority of its leaves in winter when it becomes a tangled mass of thin, untidy stems. It starts to sprout new growth in mid to late spring at which time the plant can be tidied up by trimming the old (and mostly dead) growth back to a good bud. Keep the plant well fed and watered and it will flower all summer. A less vigorous white variety *P.* 'Alba' is also available.

Rose
Perennial
Roses come in all shapes and sizes and almost all colours (the exceptions being black and blue). They grow well in containers provided that they have sufficient root room and that their soil does not remain waterlogged; they also need at least partial sunlight for a few hours each day.

During the growing season roses need lots of water and regular feeding with specified rose fertilizer. Roses need pruning at different times depending on their type.

Miniature roses are tiny replicas of normal-sized roses. They have been bred specially to be grown in pots and small containers such as windowboxes and will grow to between 9in (23cm) and 15in (38cm) tall. The flowers themselves are about 2in (5cm) across. Trim them back while they are dormant between autumn and early spring.

Patio roses make slightly larger plants and are classified as dwarf cluster-flowered bushes. They grow up to 18in (45cm) high and are most useful in individual containers or as part of a mixed planting. They are too big for windowboxes. Prune patio roses at the same time as miniatures between late autumn and early spring.

Hybrid Tea roses have large showy flowers on the end of long stems which appear in flushes. They can be grown in containers provided that they do not grow too tall — no higher than about 3ft (1m). Prune them during the dormant autumn-spring period.

Floribunda roses will flower continuously in a good summer with numerous flower heads on the same stem. The flowers themselves are smaller than Hybrid Teas but make up in numbers of flowers for the size of bloom. These, too, will grow well in containers provided that they are not tall-growing varieties. Prune them between late autumn and early spring.

Climbing roses will grow successfully provided that you choose varieties that are not too vigorous. They also need big containers and room to grow. Their stiff upright stems need to be tied to supports or they will whip around in even the lightest breeze. Climbers unlike the other roses need pruning in early winter.

Rambling roses are not the ideal roses to grow in containers as they are extremely thorny and often very vigorous. However, should a barrier plant be required, there is surely none more beautiful. They bear large cluster flowers which in many varieties develop attractive hips in late summer. If they have to be pruned, do so in late summer or

early autumn. However, this will entail losing many of the hips which are an attractive feature in winter.

Solanum jasminodes 'Album'
Perennial climber
Deciduous in all but the most sheltered positions, this white-flowered member of the potato family is surely one of the prettiest climbers of all. It produces heads of smallish, star-shaped flowers with a tiny central bright yellow boss from late spring right through until the first frosts. There are also mauve and purple varieties but these are altogether more vigorous and therefore less suited to container growing.

Snowdrop/*Galanthus nivalis*
Spring bulb
One of the most welcome flowers of the year the tiny snowdrop will grow well in pots. Grow them where they

can be admired as you go in and out of doors, or in a windowbox when they can be seen from inside. These amenable little plants will grow in sun or partial shade but don't like being waterlogged. Try to buy fresh bulbs — known as 'in the green' because dried-off bulbs often don't revive. After flowering, split the bulbs and replant immediately, continuing to water and feed until the leaves die down.

Tobacco plant/*Nicotiana affinis*
Half hardy annual
Cheerful summer and autumn flowering annuals, the unassuming tobacco plant appears in a wide range of colours — including reds, pinks, whites and pale greens — and grows to about 2.5ft (75cm) high. The trumpet-shaped flowers are 3in (8cm) long and carry a light scent. In a sun-less summer it can be near autumn before they flower.

Waterlily/*Nymphaea*
Perennial
The ordinary water lily is too big and vigorous for container culture but the miniature varieties — such as *Nymphaea tetragona* 'Alba' — which only grows to 12in (30cm) are wholly suitable. It has small dark

green floating leaves and small star-shaped single white flowers intermittently throughout summer. 'Helvola' has olive green leaves and semi-double yellow flowers. Go to a specialist water plant supplier to discover the full range of miniature waterlilies. Grow miniatures in at least 3in (8cm) of clean still water in an open, sunny position.

Arum lily/*Zantedeschia aethiopica*
Half-hardy perennial
A stately water-loving plant, the arum lily most enjoys a position in the full sun but with a moist rich soil. Very successful in a container, it will, in time with regular feeding and good culture, form a large and spectacular clump. The large grass-green arrow-shaped leaves grow to about 3ft (1m) high and die down for winter, reappearing like spears through the soil when the weather warms up in spring. The long lasting flowers (technically called spathes) appear from late spring into summer, and resemble a crisp white sheet of paper curled around a central yellow prong.

Hebe
Evergreen perennial shrub
Hebes are grown as much for their foliage as their flowers, which are in the blue/purple/mauve and white range in summer and autumn. There is a good range from which to choose; some are small, compact,

low-growing plants, while other varieties grow into medium-sized shrubs. The former make good windowbox plants, but not the latter. Grow them instead in tubs and larger containers. Check the size and spread of the plant before buying. Although evergreen they enjoy good sunshine and protection from cold winter winds. Grow them in a good multi-purpose or soil-based compost and crock the container well as they react badly to waterlogged soil.

INFORMATIVE & INSPIRATIONAL IDEAS FOR CONTAINER GARDENING

Red

Right: Massed blocks of spring tulips give a greater intensity of colour than any other plant at this time of the year.

Below: Red geraniums are almost a cliche in container gardening because they are such reliable and colourful plants; even a novice gardener can produce a magnificent display.

Begonia
Tuberous perennial
Begonias are one of the most useful plants for hanging baskets and windowboxes, as their naturally lax habit makes them ideal for viewing from below. On the whole they are not subtle — often big and blowzy in strong colours. They flower reliably with no more than regular care and attention. Their juicy stems are loved by slugs and snails but this is not a problem for hanging baskets!

Dahlia
Half-hardy tuberous perennial
A large and diverse family of brightly flowering plants most of which are really too big and vigorous for container growing. However there are plenty of the smaller varieties, notably the dwarf forms, which make good pot subjects. Grow them in good, well drained multi purpose

compost in a sunny position. Their fleshy shoots make them a target for aphids. The first frost will blacken and shrivel their foliage, so at the first sign of winter dig up the tubers, shake off the soil, cut all the stems down to 1in (2.5cm) above the tuber and store the tubers somewhere dry and frost free. Plant out the following spring after the danger of frost has passed.

Monkey Flower/*Mimulus*
Annual
These easily grown plants (actually perennials but usually grown as annuals) make useful windowbox subjects as they only grow to about 6in (15cm) high. The plants grow rapidly, branching out to produce masses of flowers in pink, red, yellow or orange throughout summer. Grow them in multi-purpose compost and give them a sunny spot and plenty of water after hot days. Although fiddly, it help flower production if the spent flower heads are removed.

Rhododendron
Shrub
Always a popular plant for spring colour, the rhododendron can grow into a large shrub up to 6ft (2m) high and wide given sufficient root room. Most rhododendrons have large evergreen leaves which set off their huge clustered flower heads of purples, reds, pinks, white or pale lemon which appear in spring and

early summer. Rhododendrons are especially valuable for filling shady areas where other plants would struggle for sufficient light. However, keep them away from exposure to cold winds which will blast their flower buds and young leaf growth. Grow them in either multi-purpose compost or special ericaceous compost. Keep the soil moist, ideally with rainwater in hard water areas.

Tulip
Bulb
These brightly coloured spring-flowering bulbs are a real sign that summer is not too far away. They are particularly valuable for their dazzling colours in probably the widest range that any flower can offer. Many varieties also have interestingly striped and speckled foliage which prolongs their period of interest in the garden. Grow the shorter varieties in windowboxes and the taller ones in ordinary containers in a well-drained multi-purpose compost. Grow tulips in containers and bring them into a prominent position — but out of the wind — as they burst into flower; with careful planning you can have tulips in flower from early spring right into early summer. After flowering, cut off the dead heads but continue to water and feed the bulbs and they should flower again successfully the following year. They need to be split up every three years.

Pink

Anemone
Corms/perennials
The little *Anemone blanda* is a late winter/mid-spring flowering plant ideal for windowboxes and containers as it only grows about 6in high. Its cheerful daisy-like flowers in blues, pink or white will grow happily in sun or partial shade in any ordinary compost. It is an undemanding plant which will die down and reappear the following year.

The De Caen and St Brigid series have much larger more colourful flowers and are the anemones found in florists. They appear in spring in scarlet, inky blue, purples, pinks and white. They are taller growing than their little cousins but are similarly undemanding.

Perennial garden anemones, known as Japanese anemones (*A.japonica*), flower at the end of summer in either pink or white. These are tall, up to 5ft (1.5m) high, and will rapidly swamp smaller and more delicate plants, so grow them on their own in pots.

Busy Lizzie/*Impatiens capensis*
Annual
No flowering plant is more valuable for growing in shady or partial shade conditions than the busy lizzie. Once it starts to flower it will continue to do so until the frost cuts it down or

it simply runs out of steam. Often bought as single pot plants, busy lizzies also easy to raise from seed. Because of its popularity, plant breeders are continuously improving its qualities although they have yet to break the fairly limited white, red, pink, orange and mauve colour range.

It is a fleshy plant which needs a plentiful water supply to remain healthy — unfortunately this also makes it popular with greenfly, but these are easily controlled. Busy lizzies are equally effective grown on their own or in a mixed container,

Camellia
Evergreen shrub
It looks so exotic, yet the camellia is completely hardy. The biggest problem is that the plant easily suffers blast damage to its buds if early spring sunshine burns the frost off; grow it, therefore, in an east-facing location to avoid the problem. Camellias grow well in containers and actually enjoy a semi-shaded, sheltered position. Give them well drained, neutral to acid soil (they won't grow in alkaline soil) and feed in summer. If the leaves start to yellow apply sequestrine feed to the soil. Should the plant need trimming, do so immediately after flowering. After spring flowering the camellia makes an attractive foliage plant with its oval, shiny dark green leaves.

INFORMATIVE & INSPIRATIONAL **IDEAS** FOR CONTAINER GARDENING

Cyclamen
Tuberous perennial
Small and miniature cyclamen make good subjects for sunny windowboxes and troughs. The species is completely hardy and will produce pink, purple or white flowers in massed succession in late winter and spring after which the main flush of silver-grey heart-shaped leaves appear. Give cyclamen humus-rich, well-drained soil taking care to water the surrounding soil not to soak the crown of the plant.

Diascia
Hardy annual
A small pink-flowered trailing annual, the diascia is a useful plant for windowboxes and hanging baskets. It grows to about 8in (20cm) high with heart-shaped pale green leaves and requires a sunny spot and moist multi-purpose compost. Strictly speaking a perennial, most diascias are grown as annuals but, given protection, they can survive the winter. If so, trim them back to a good bud in spring and start them into growth again.

Fuchsia
Small shrub
One of the best and most reliable of all types of plant for container growing, the only real drawback of the fuchsia is the lack of winter hardiness in most species; however, the range of hardy fuchsias is increasing all the time. There are two basic types of fuchsia — bush and trailing. The latter work best in hanging baskets and windowboxes where their dangling flowers can be seen to best advantage. Fuchsias grow most happily in light shade in a free-draining multi-purpose compost. They will flower throughout the summer months if encouraged with regular feeding. Their relatively limited colour range of reds, pinks, whites and purples appear in seemingly endless combinations in the many hundreds of named varieties. Pinch out the growing tips to encourage bushiness on the new spring growth, though this will delay flowering for about six weeks.

Hydrangea
Perennial shrub
Hydrangeas are much more than just seaside plants and make extremely useful and attractive container plants, especially where a large area needs filling. There are many different species but only two types are suitable for containers: mophead (Hortensias) and lacecap — the others are too vigorous. Even then mophead and lacecap hydrangeas will grow to a good 6ft (2m) high and wide. Hydrangea flowers appear in white, pinks, purples and a startlingly bright blue, their colour depending on the soil in which they are grown. The blue and purple

Opposite page: The elegant Cyclamen persicum flourishes through the winter months into spring, being ideally suited to shady conditions.

Below: Zonal geraniums often possess attractively marked leaves. Keep them in the sunshine for the best colouration.

Above: Fuchsias grow in two main forms — bushy and upright or lax and trailing. The latter are seen to best advantage in hanging baskets and windowboxes.

Right: Busy lizzies have many virtues which makes them one of the most useful of all container plants. The plants flower in profusion all summer until the autumn frosts and cold air cut them down and they will happily grow in a shady position and still flower continuously.

INFORMATIVE &
INSPIRATIONAL
IDEAS FOR
CONTAINER
GARDENING

flowers need an acid soil to retain their colouring, otherwise they will appear as a muddy purpley-pink; red or pink flowers need a neutral or alkaline soil. Hydrangeas grow well in partial shade in well-drained soil. In containers they need frequent watering in hot weather or they will collapse.

Lavatera/Mallow
Annual and perennial shrub
Although a large growing shrub, Lavateria will grow in containers provided it lives in a large pot of good compost (such as John Innes No 3) and are well fed and watered. Bushes have silver-grey, slightly furry leaves and white, pink or dark maroon flowers in the summer.

Oleander/*Nerium oleander*
Perennial shrub
A highly poisonous but very attractive pink, white or red flowered Mediterranean shrub. oleanders are not fully hardy and require protection from the frosts though they will survive in sheltered positions outside in a mild winter. Oleanders grow well in containers provided that they are well watered and fed, and sit in as sunny a position as possible. Cut back their lanky growth to encourage bushiness and more flowers which will appear throughout the summer in clusters at the tips of the branches.

Oxalis
Small perennial
Grow oxalis on its own or its invasiveness can throttle other more tentative plants — its tiny, rather radish-like tubers spread rapidly and can be hard to extract from among other roots. Oxalis leaves look like clover and their flat flowers appear in pinks and purples in the summer. They can take full sun or partial shade but need a well-drained multi-purpose compost.

Geranium (Pelargonium)
Tender perennial
The quintessential pot plant, the tender geranium is correctly known as a pelargonium. Of the most popular cultivated types, there are four most commonly found — three grown primarily for their flowers and one mostly for its leaves. They all thrive in the sunshine and need protection from cold and damp in winter.

Geraniums have a fairly limited colour range of whites, pinks and reds plus a few mauves but the range and combination of colours within that list is is enormous. None of them grow very big, so they are ideal for container culture. Feed and water all geraniums regularly: with good cultivation they are largely trouble-free. Remove spent flower heads as they go over to ensure the continuous production of flower buds.

Zonal Pelargoniums are the commonest type which will flower reliably. Some zonals have interestingly marked leaves but they are usually grown for their flowers. Fleshy upright stems can grow up to 3ft (1m) or more high in some varieties, but are usually more like 18in (46cm) in height and spread. Their colour range is red, pink and white with some so-called oranges. Dwarf varieties are being increasingly hybridised, particularly with windowbox culture in mind. Like all geraniums they need protection in winter although they will survive outside in a protected position during a mild winter.

Pelargonium peltatum is the ivy-leaved trailing geranium which is so useful for hanging baskets and windowboxes. It is a brittle plant and so needs careful handling; some varieties can be a bit whispy but others — especially the continental trailers — will form an impressive mass of leaves and flowers. Mauve-flowered varieties are available as well as the usual geranium colours. In all respects treat *P. peltatum* the same way as zonal pelargoniums

Pelargonium x domesticum is better known as the regal pelargonium; this has larger, more showy, flowers but not produced as generously. They are striking plants when in flower but are harder to

flower successfully and need to be kept in warmer winter conditions than the others.

Scented pelargoniums — there are a number of different named species which are all grown for their fragrant leaves which can smell of anything from lemons and oranges to roses,pine, peppermint and even chocolate. These plants still flower but the blooms tend to be small and — while pretty — fairly insignificant.

Verbena
Annual
A member of a large plant family, the trailing verbena is another very useful plant for hanging baskets and windowboxes. Give it a good sunny position and plenty of water and fertilizer throughout the summer. Verbena dislike drying out and will rapidly stop flowering and lose their leaves if neglected. Remove the dead flower heads to keep them flowering.

Blue

Above: Swan River Daisies are usually blue but they can also be pink or white. Their finely cut foliage gives them a rather misty appearance. As here they combine well with felicia.

Right: Lacecap hydrangeas make good container plants and in the course of a few seasons will grow quite large. The blue varieties are particularly striking but may need chemical help to retain their intensity of colour.

INFORMATIVE &
INSPIRATIONAL
IDEAS FOR
CONTAINER
GARDENING

Agapanthus
Perennial
Probably the loveliest of all the summer-flowering bulbs, the stately agapanthus thrives in a pot in a sunny situation. Unfortunately they are not all reliably hardy but some garden varieties — such as the Headbourne Hybrids — will survive most winters in a sheltered position. Multiple flower heads appear like huge pom-poms on the end of elegantly slim stems rising above their long, strap-like leaves. The flowers — which open in mid to late summer — have a blue intensity which really makes them stand out. There are also white varieties which are equally attractive but less striking.

Swan River Daisy/Brachycome
Annual
The Swan River Daisy has delicate pretty little blue daisy-like flowers all summer held above feathery foliage. It grows to around 18in (45cm) high and comes in white and pink as well as the commoner blues and purples. It enjoys a sheltered sunny position with free-draining compost and not too much water. It is easily flattened by rain and wind.

Campanula
Annual, bi-annual
This is a truly blue family of easily grown plants. Some are low-growing and upright, others trail and others still grow into tall plants. They grow happily in sun or partial sun in any type of compost: the smaller types are best for container culture. Larger campanulas have the disadvantage of having one spectacular flowering period of two or three weeks and then nothing but foliage. *C. isophyllia* is a most attractive but tender trailing variety with blue, purple or white flowers. *C. carpatica* is a similar-flowered but non-trailing species. Both will flower continuously provided their spent flower heads are removed as they die.

Felicia
Perennial
This little daisy-flowered plant will flower in profusion all summer long provided the dead flower heads are snipped off. Hardy through mild winters in a sheltered position it is really valuable container plant which really deserves to be better known. A variegated leaf variety is also available.

Grape Hyacinth/Muscari
Bulb
Spring-flowering small bulbs, the flower spikes often appear before the long, strap-shaped leaves. Give them a sunny spot in a pot containing well-drained soil. Let them die down without disturbance and they will appear again the following year. They are ideal for growing under deciduous shrubs where they can flower before the larger plant comes into leaf.

Lobelia
Annual
The backbone of many container
arrangements, the tiny-flowered
lobelia fills any awkward gaps with its
feathery green foliage and profusion
of flowers. Grown mostly in either
Oxford (dark) or Cambridge (light)
blue, it also flowers in pink and white
shades. Although easily raised from
seed, it is most often bought as 2in
(5cm) high plantlets. Be aware that
the shorter upright growing variety is
also offered in the same way, so if you
want trailing lobelia check that that is
what you are buying.

Morning Glory/*Ipomoea tricolor*
Annual climber
The morning glory is one of the
easiest and most spectacular vines of
all to grow with its sky-blue, trumpet
shaped flowers which open on sunny
mornings and close up after mid-day.
Easily raised from seed, it requires
some sort of support over which it
can twine its way up to as much as
8ft (2.4m). Grow morning glory in
the sunshine in rich, well-drained soil
and keep it well watered and fed
throughout the summer. Grow a
number of plants together in the
same container to get a good size
spread. It is not frost-hardy and will
die with the first autumn frosts.

Phlox
Hardy perennial
The taller herbaceous phloxes are not
suitable for container culture, but the
smaller, lower growing species can be.
The flowers come in a wide range of
colours and are often scented. Grow
them in a sunny or only lightly
shaded position, in a good, rich
multi-purpose compost which is free
draining. Dead-head spent flowers
regularly; taller growth may well need
staking to prevent the heavy flower
heads drooping.

Plumbago/*Plumbago auriculata*
Tender perennial
Although a Mediterranean shrub the
plumbago will grow and flower
enthusiastically given reasonable
amounts of sunshine. It sends out
long arching shoots from which
clusters of powder blue flowers
appear from summer through until
autumn. A white-flowered variety is
equally vigorous but can be a little
harder to find. Within a couple of
growing seasons and given a large
container, the plumbago will get to
be a middling size shrub. Its
drawback is that it need complete
protection from the frost in winter
— it must be taken indoors — but
all it needs is to be frost-free, an
unheated porch will suffice in all but
the hardest winters.

INFORMATIVE &
INSPIRATIONAL
IDEAS FOR
CONTAINER
GARDENING

Far left: The African lily or agapanthus is magnificent in containers, especially when it has matured into a clump. Largely trouble-free they do require protection from winter wet and cold.

Left: *Felicia amelloides* is a small bushy perennial which trails gently and flowers continuously throughout the summer as long as the dead flower heads are regularly removed. It enjoys a sunny position and regular watering.

Purple

Above: Purple verbena and variegated ivy make this pot into an eye-catching feature.

INFORMATIVE &
INSPIRATIONAL
IDEAS FOR
CONTAINER
GARDENING

Clematis
Perennial climber
A large and diverse family of mostly climbing plants — with careful planning you can have one of the family in flower all year round. Between them clematis offer almost every permutation possible: evergreen/deciduous, large flowered/small-flowered, hardy/tender, spring/summer/autumn/winter flowering.

Broadly speaking, the species clematis are smaller and more profuse-flowering as well as more vigorous than the hybrids which have much bigger, flashier but fewer flowers. Clematis also split into spring or summer flowering. Whichever you have, they all need to have their roots in the shade otherwise they are likely to die. Give all types of clematis a wall or some support up which to grow so their leaf stalks can attach themselves by twining. Do not grow clematis in plastic pots as these do not provide sufficient insulation from the heat in summer nor the cold in winter. Use instead wood, stone, terracotta or ceramic containers. The pot must be large: at least 45cm deep and 30–40cm in diameter, with plenty of drainage holes, and filled with John Innes No 3. Clematis notoriously like to have their roots in shade and their heads in the sun. Give them also a large container where their roots can run. Some clematis are just not suitable for container growing: look for varieties which are naturally compact and bushy so their growth doesn't get over-exuberant for your patio.

Spring flowering early season clematis flower on the previous year's growth and so need to be pruned just after flowering or all the following year's flowers will be lost. *C. montana*, the familiar pink or white flowered climber which smothers whatever it is growing over in early spring is too vigorous for pot culture. Look instead for smaller growing varieties which are less exuberant; *C. alpina* has exquisite blue flowers and makes an absolute picture, but sadly only for a short time — a considerable drawback if you only have a limited area in which to grow plants. Try some of the larger early flowering cultivars such as 'Masquerade', Pink Champagne', and 'Ruby Glow'.

Summer flowering larger-flowered hybrid clematis come into their own when the sunshine starts to be reliable. With the later-flowering varieties, flowers form on the new growth, so all the top growth should be pruned back in early spring to force the flowers to appear lower down the plant where they can be admired. There are many popular varieties in a huge range of colours, again choose less vigorous, more compact varieties.

Cup and Saucer Vine/
Cobaea scandens
Half hardy perennial climber
The Cup and Saucer Vine is a
vigorous climber that needs a big
container and plenty of water in a
good sunny position. It also requires
a wall or trellis work for its tendrils to
cling onto — well treated it can grow
to as much as 20ft (6m) in a long
summer season. It will not survive
cold winter weather. Cobaea has large
initially green flowers which become
purpley-blue, or more rarely white,
bell-shaped flowers and large mid
green lobed leaves. Grow in a
sheltered position in the full sun in
deep rich multi-purpose compost or
John Innes No 3; water well but don't
feed or it will just put on leaf growth
at the expense of flowers. Dead-head
the spent flowers to encourage more
buds.

Heather/Erica
Small perennial evergreen shrub
In late summer to early winter the
heathers come into flower in shades
of purple, mauve and white. They
make especially good windowbox
plants as they do not grow high
enough to obscure the view from
inside the house — only about
12–18in (30–45cm) with the same
spread. Their most important
requirement is ericaceous compost —
ie, compost that is lime free — which
can be bought in special bags at
garden centres and nurseries. They

enjoy the sunshine and need to be
kept well watered.

Heathers traditionally have dark
green, needle-shaped leaves, but there
are plenty of varieties with bright
green, silver-grey or golden foliage.

Hibiscus/*Hibiscus syriacus*
Deciduous shrub
The hardy hibiscus is an attractive
late summer to autumn flowering
shrub which needs to be grow in a
large container if it is to thrive. It is
not truly an ideal container plant as
for a good five months of the year it
is leafless; its prime virtue is that it
flowers profusely at a time when
relatively few other plants are
performing. Hibiscus make an
attractive, neat shape and only need
pruning if they get too big. The
flowers are mainly combinations of
white and pink, single or double and
up to 4in (10cm) in diameter. The
most striking variety is 'Blue Bird'
with large bluey-purple flowers.

Iris
Bulb
Only the smaller species are suitable
for container culture — Iris
histrioides and I. reticulata. The
former is only 4in (10cm) high with
bright blue flowers in winter
(however the leaves do grow much
higher in summer) and is a welcome
sight during the grey months of the
year. *I. reticulata* flowers a bit later in
early spring with purple-blue flowers.

It also grows a little higher – to 6in
(15cm). Both species enjoy sunshine
but are tough enough to cope with
winter conditions.

Lavender/Lavandula
Small perennial shrub
The many varieties of lavender are
indispensable for a container garden,
what with the beauty of their flowers
and the spicy aromatic aroma of their
silver-grey foliage. Lavender
withstand drought well provided
their roots have plenty of room (a
big container) and relish the sunshine
— after all they are Mediterranean
plants. Bushes need to grow in well
drained multi purpose or soil based
compost: a well grown plant will get
to be 3–4ft (1–1.2m) high.

Lavender can grow straggly so it
requires a light trim after flowering,
but don't cut too far down or it will
cause die-back. The characteristic
purple or blue flowers open in
midsummer and last on the bush into
autumn all the while attracting bees
and hoverflies.

Pansy
Hardy annual
These cheerful little plants grow
happily in containers and provide a
wide range of colours from which to
choose. Remove spent flowerheads to
encourage the growth of more buds.
They enjoy the sunshine but will still
grow in partial shade and will flower
provided that they get some sun.

Above: Little violas flower much more freely than their larger cousins the pansies.

Right: One of the most successful plants for hanging baskets is bidens. Each plant is rather sparse, so a lot need to be planted together to get a full effect.

Summer pansies are one of the truly old-fashioned flowers with their cheerful little 'faces' and bright range of colours. Easily grown and undemanding they make good container plants especially in windowboxes where their restricted height makes they very useful.

Winter pansies are also known as 'Universal' pansies, have been specially bred to cope with lower winter temperatures, though they need to be sheltered from strong winds and rain which damage the flowers. They are sold for immediate planting as young plants in the autumn and are ideal for winter windowboxes and containers as not much else will be flowering at the same time. As yet their colour range is not as wide as the summer flowering pansies, namely mainly purples, deep violet and yellow usually with black markings.

Petunia
Annual
Along with lobelia and geraniums, petunias make up the great triumvirate of container plants. But, unlike the others, petunias come in a huge range of colours — white, reds, pinks, yellows, blues and purples — often striped or throated in darker shades or in completely contrasting white. Buy them in harlequin mixtures for a multi-coloured effect, or limit yourself to one or two for an actual colour scheme.

Petunias are usually sold as either multiflora — small flowers but lots of them, or grandiflora which have fewer but bigger flowers. Also in the last five years or so trailing petunias have become available and have transformed hanging baskets everywhere with their cascades of flowers, although in a limited colour range as yet. The trailing 'Surfina' petunias have transformed hanging baskets in recent years with their tumbling profusions of flowers all summer. Their only drawback is the relatively limited colour range — they do not yet come in the full petunia range, but hybridists are constantly working to 'break' new colour forms.

Viola
Annual
Similar to pansies in looks but very much smaller altogether, the violas are very pretty little plants which flower prolifically in late winter and throughout spring. Available in a good colour range they will flower continuously if regularly dead-headed. Their ideal situation is in the semi shade in well drained but well watered multi compost. Treat them in the same way as Universal pansies.

INFORMATIVE &
INSPIRATIONAL
IDEAS FOR
CONTAINER
GARDENING

Yellow

Abutilon

Half hardy perennial

Abutilon megapotanicum is a rather lax, slimly stemmed shrub with maple-like leaves and small pendulous dark red and yellow bell-shaped flowers. It is hardy in a sheltered sunny position provided it has a good free-draining compost, but it will need the support of a stout cane or tying in to a wall or trellis. Feed regularly in the growing season but watch particularly for aphid and scale insect attack. *A.x hybridium* is somewhat sturdier, more tender and has large bell-shaped flowers in shades or red, orange and yellow.

Another abutilon species, *A.pictum* is grown for its variegated yellow and green leaves and not for its unremarkable flowers. It is not tender and is best treated as an annual unless it can be given winter protection from frost.

Calendula/*Calendula officinalis*

Annual

The pot marigold — the name says it all! This plant shines out in yellows, golds and oranges from its surrounds. Easily grown from seed the pot marigold has a distinct aroma redolent of cottage gardens. The flower petals can be used in salads for taste as well as decoration.

Chrysanthemum

Perennial

A very popular autumn flowering plant, pot-grown chrysanthemums are usually treated with a chemical retardant to stop them from growing too tall. This wears off in their second season which explains why your 12in (30.4cm) high plant one year become a 3ft (0.9m) plus giant the next. First year plants are ideal for windowboxes but in subsequent seasons will need to be moved to a larger, ground-based container.

Chrysanthemums come in a wide colour range encompassing yellows, bronzes, oranges, reds and pinks. Grow in good light conditions in free-draining soil out of the wind, stake taller plants. Feed them every week from mid to late summer; cut down the spent autumn growth and protect young shoots from the frost in spring.

Cotton lavender/*Santolina chamaecyparissus*

Perennial shrub

A useful arching plant, cotton lavender forms neat mounds of grey-green leaves and small button-shaped yellow flowers in summer. Its growth can get very straggly, so cut it back to a good shoot in spring but being careful not to cut into the old wood.

Santolina is a Mediterranean plant so grow it where it can get plenty of sunshine in free-draining multi-purpose compost or John Innes No 2. Cut off the spent flower heads and trim the more straggly shoots back to shape.

Above: The yellow Dutch crocus (*Crocus x luteus*) is a welcome reminder that spring is on the way and it is time to start thinking about your summer pots and planting schemes.

Right: Massed daffodils such as *Narcissus* 'Peeping Tom' will give the impression of a country garden even in the heart of the city.

INFORMATIVE & INSPIRATIONAL **IDEAS** FOR CONTAINER GARDENING

Crocus
Bulb
Some of the very earliest flowers of the year belong to the crocus. Different species flower at various times but in a limited range of colours — white, purple, mauve, yellow and orange. Put them in a sunny position where they will be encouraged to open out their flowers.

Crocus are ideal for small containers on their own or mixed in with evergreens such as ivies and box, to give a splash of colour. Buy them as bulbs in autumn for immediate planting — with careful selection you can keep a range of crocus flowering from late winter right through spring. They can be left in position after flowering and just watered and fed with the plants around them.

Daffodil
Bulb
Only the miniature daffodils are really suitable for windowbox culture but many of the ordinary species and varieties are ideal for growing in containers. There are many different types to choose from varying from tiny 2in (2cm) high plants to 18in (45cm), and in colour from yellow of differing hues, to whites, creams and oranges. Plant them in early autumn to twice their diameter in depth into well drained multi-purpose compost and position their container in the sun. After flowering cut off the dead heads but leave the foliage to die

back naturally for a minimum of six weeks if you want them to flower the following year (during which time they must be fed with fertilizer). Alternatively plant them out in a border or discard the bulbs.

Honeysuckle/Lonicera
Climber
If you have the room grow a honeysuckle — better yet two — make sure that they are one of the scented varieties. There are many types to choose from with flowers ranging from the tiny to 4in (10cm) long. The flower colours are mostly yellows, lemons, oranges and creams, sometimes flushed with vivid pink. Some varieties are extremely vigorous so not really ideal for container growing, look for less exuberant varieties. A few species are evergreen but most are deciduous and start shooting in early spring with the first sunshine.

Grow honeysuckle in a good strong soil based compost such as John Innes No 3 and position them against a wall or trellis where they will get the sun — like clematis, honeysuckle likes its roots in the shade where they will stay moist.
Summer flowering honeysuckle — *Lonicera periclymenum* — is the commonest honeysuckle with a fragrant scent and vigorous habit. However there are plenty of others which will reward you with good growth and lots of flowers.

Winter flowering honeysuckle — *L. fragrantissima* — flowers from early winter with strongly scented creamy white flowers. Although generally deciduous, in mild positions it will remain more or less evergreen. Not as rampant as many of its cousins winter honeysuckle only grows in maturity to around 6ft (2m).

Hyacinth/*Hyacinthus orientalis*
Spring bulb
For a scented patio or windowbox in spring, no plant can beat the heady unmistakable perfume of the hyacinth. Buy and plant the bulbs in autumn and they will start to appear with the sunshine in early spring. As well as purple, they come in blue, white, pink, red, apricot and yellow. Their large flowerheads sometimes flop and need support when they are grown in low light conditions.

Discard the bulbs after flowering as they will perform very poorly the following year, so if you have a garden, dig them into the border, otherwise just throw them away.

Lantana
Tender perennial
A plant much relished by butterflies, the lantana needs a sunny, reasonably sheltered position in well drained soil. The plant can get leggy and will benefit from regular pinching out to encourage the side shoots to sprout. Too tender to cope with a British winter, the lantana will need protection from the frost and cold to survive into a second season.

Polyanthus/Primula
Hardy perennial
There are many different types of primula in the widest range possible of colours, happily almost all the species and varieties are suitable for container growing. Indeed many of the alpines are particularly adapted for growing in a trough or windowbox where their low growing habit makes them ideal.

The best known member of the primula family is the lovely primrose from which garden polyanthus have been hybridized. These flower in an enormous range of colours during the spring months. Grow them in the sunshine and cut off the spent flower heads regularly and they will keep going until the early summer flowers start. Grow them in multi-purpose compost and keep them moist — if they dry out they rapidly collapse.

Ranunculus
Hardy perennial
Huge blowzy members of the buttercup family, ranunculus are increasingly appearing as mid spring flowers in the markets and garden

centres. Their bright colours — pink, orange, yellow, white and red — catch the eye wherever they are planted. A little too tall for windowboxes, they will do well in larger containers in multi-purpose compost provided they are kept moist and dead headed regularly.

Sedum
Perennial
Another huge family with a wide variety of habit, although not by any means all are suitable for container growing. Sedums are all succulents, so require a sunny position in well drained multi-purpose compost: the smaller species like stonecrop grow well in a trough where they will trail over the edge in time.

In autumn the magenta flat-headed flowers of the iceplant, *S. spectabile* attract butterflies every bit as much as the buddleia does, and for this reason alone it is worth growing provided you have the room.

In winter the plant will die down completely to just a few grey-green shoots at ground level.

Spurge/Euphorbia
Hardy annual, perennial
The euphorbias are a huge plant family with characteristic spurge-like growth. They all contain a milky sap which contains a skin irritant that causes blisters, so they are plants to be avoided if children are likely to come into contact with them or people with sensitive skins. In any case be very careful when handling them yourself.

Of the many different species, *E.wulfenii* has bluey-green strap-like leaves and bright yellow flower heads, alternatively *E.griffithii* has flame red flowers (although actually these are bracts, a type of false leaf). After the summer cut back the growth to within a few inches of the soil.

INFORMATIVE & INSPIRATIONAL **IDEAS** FOR CONTAINER GARDENING

Orange

Campsis
Perennial climber
Although properly a warm climate plant the campsis is hardy in most of the south of Britain in sheltered positions. This rampant climber gives a true touch of the exotic with its trumpet-shaped orangey-red flowers that appear in the late summer and autumn. Given a sunny position and plenty of water and fertilizer it is a vigorous vine which needs the support of a wall or trellis. Campsis loose their leaves in winter and only start to regrow new shoots when the weather warms up in spring.

Canna
Tender rhizome
For an exotic effect it takes a lot to beat the canna or Indian shot plant — now coming back into fashion after a long absence. Anything from 2–6ft (0.6–1.8m) or more tall, the canna throws out a number of large paddle-shaped leaves which are attractive in themselves, in dark or bright green, dark purple, cream striped, or a mixture of all in the variety 'Durban'. Multiple flowers appear on top of tall stems in bright shades of red, pink, yellow, apricot and orange — they are not for the faint-hearted!

Cannas are not hardy and need protection from frosts and damp in winter. The first frost will wither their leaves, after this cut the stems back to about 4in (10cm) above the soil level and bring them inside to a shed or garage to dry out and overwinter. Otherwise cannas can be left in their containers and stored in a dry, frost-free place. Start them again in fresh multi-purpose compost in spring in a warm position. Do not put cannas outside until the weather warms up. Feed and water regularly throughout the growing season.

Nasturtium/ *Tropaeolum majus*
Annual
One of the very easiest of flowers to raise from seed, nasturtiums are also sold as ready-to-plant seedlings. Their slightly fleshy, spicy smelling foliage is used by some people in green salads — as are their colourful flowers. Nasturtiums climb and trail over and along anything they can reach provided they get lots of sunshine, furthermore, as they grow quickly they are very useful for covering unsightly objects. They are also the exception to the rule about compost — ordinary garden soil suits them fine — a good compost will provide them with too much food and they will just grow leaves at the expense of flowers. However, still feed them with a weak liquid fertilizer every fortnight. The flowers themselves come in shades of reds, oranges, yellows and creams followed by peppery tasting seed heads in clusters of three. Keep nasturtiums well watered or they will wilt and turn yellow. Their biggest problem by far is black fly which start as a few black specks on the underside of the leaves. These rapidly multiply until the plant is entirely disfigured with aphids. Inspect and spray your nasturtiums even more rigorously than your other plants, however, by keeping them well watered and healthy they are far less likely to attract trouble.

Above: The colourful effect of this imposing container is entirely derived from foliage. Purple-leaved sage at the top, lemon thyme in the middle and trailing variegated catmint completes the simple but effective planting.

Right: Japanese maples are grown for the exaggerated shape and extraordinary colour of their leaves — which often intensifies in autumn.

INFORMATIVE &
INSPIRATIONAL
IDEAS FOR
CONTAINER
GARDENING

Foliage

Acer/Japanese Maple
Deciduous tree
There are many different types of acer, however for container culture choose one of the smaller species. All have attractive jagged-edge leaves in greens, creams or dark purples but it is for their autumn colour that they are especially valued. At this time the leaves explode into brilliant fiery reds, bronzes and oranges (depending on variety). All acers are slow growing — notoriously so — which explains why they are so expensive to buy. Grow them in sun or partial shade in a large container containing a good loam based compost such as John Innes No 3. Keep the plant well watered and moist and out of prevailing winds. Mulch the surface of the compost in spring with a good propriety mix.

Agave
Tender perennial
Redolent of sun drenched Mediterranean gardens, the agave needs lots of sun, plenty of room to grow and shelter from cold winds. In maturity the agave becomes a spiky architectural plant with huge fleshy leaves unfolding from a central crown. Some varieties have a cream variegated stripe. Agave must have protection from the cold winds and frosts, otherwise it will quickly shrivel and die. Grow it in a free-draining, good loam based compost, well weighted at the bottom to provide stability.

Lady's Mantle/*Alchemilla mollis*
Hardy perennial
A charming low-growing primarily foliage plant, although it does have dense clusters of greeny-yellow flowers in summer. However it is for the silver-green velvety leaves that it is treasured. To call it a 'filler' does not do it justice — although few plants do the job better or more prettily.

Alchemilla arches attractively over the edges of pots and containers which makes it very useful for growing underneath larger plants which produce a length of bare stem. It will grow in almost any conditions as long as the compost is free-draining.

Bamboo
Perennial
Another candidate for the exotic-effect patio, the bamboo is actually a type of particularly tough grass. Although quick growing, bamboo can be slow to establish, so big plants are expensive. However nothing works as well as a screen, whether from the neighbours, unattractive views or winds. Beware though, because they are so big they are gross feeders and require lots of water in hot weather as well as regular feeding. The leaves rapidly wilt when the plant is dry, but they do pick up again quickly provided they haven't been left dry for too long.

There are many different species varying in heights from 10in (25cm) or so, to 20ft (6m) — choose wisely.

Some have green stems (properly called culms), others yellow, black or striped. Bamboo is very easy to look after and is largely trouble-free. It looses some of its leaves in winter.

Box/*Buxus sempervirens*
Shrub
Box is the very best plant for creating a topiary garden — although slow-growing it is remarkably amenable to shaping. Arguably it looks its best in winter with the frosts and snow delineating its form. Easily grown, box nevertheless needs free-draining but humus-rich compost. Apply a weak liquid feed from late spring to late summer. For topiary specimens, clip to shape in late summer/early autumn.

The commonest variety is *Buxus sempervirens*, which in time will grow up to as much as 10ft (3m) in the open soil, but rather less in containers — a larger container will sustain a larger plant. There are variegated varieties with yellow or white ('gold' or 'silver') variegation which also make attractive plants, but they are even slower growing!

Fatsia/Castor Oil Plant
Shrub
One of the very easiest of all plants to grow in a container, the huge glossy green leaves give a distinctly tropical look, but nevertheless it is bone hardy. The castor oil plant has everything a gardener can reasonably ask. Even quite small plants bloom with huge

heads of tiny white flowers. Extremely adaptable, the castor oil plant can fill a shady corner or sit happily in the sunshine. Given a large container it will grow quite big within a few years.

Ornamental Cabbage/*Brassica oleracea*
Annual
The ornamental cabbage — green, yellow, pink, cream and white — has appeared as a pot plant in recent years. Completely hardy, its prime appeal is as a provider of winter colour, however the tips of the leaves can be browned by frost if the plant is too exposed. Mature plants go to seed at which time they look straggly and unattractive and are best thrown away.

Eucalyptus
Tree
Although a big tree in its native Australia, *E. gunnii* can be grown in a large container provided that it is well fed and watered, and regularly cut

back hard. Its young growth produces unusual aromatic silvery-grey disk-like leaves which are ideal for flower arranging.

Eucalyptus growth will be restricted due to being grown in a container, so to prevent the plant from 'suffering' make sure it is well watered and fed to keep it healthy. Continue to repot the tree as needed until it reaches the desired size, then in future, trim the branches quite hard to contain its growth.

Euphorbia/Spurge
Perennial
Easy-to grow plant of which there are many different types. All have yellow, green or red flowers. One of the most popular varieties is *E. charasias wulfenii* with greeny-blue leaves and yellow summer flowers. All the spurges contain a milky sap which can cause skin problems, so this is not a plant to grow where children are likely to be playing.

Above: *Agave americana* **'Marginata' is a splendid plant for Mediterranean style patios. Place it well away from pathways as the spikes can be lethal! They also need protection from winter frosts and cold weather.**

Right: Clipped box is in many ways the ideal plant — and it looks especially good when covered in frost and snow.

INFORMATIVE & INSPIRATIONAL IDEAS FOR CONTAINER GARDENING

Ferns
Hardy perennial

For moist, fairly dark, cool positions ferns are sometimes the only answer, but what a reply! Their subtle green elegance will enhance an otherwise dreary corner. Given such conditions they are easy to grow and give virtually no trouble. Avoid the tender ferns, and instead look for some of the many hardy species to choose from — from the tiniest alpines to the largest plants.

One of the definitions of a fern is that it doesn't flower, instead they have spores — brown 'furry' dots on the undersides of their leaves — with which they reproduce.

For container culture avoid the more vigorous species, and be sure to keep the soil moist. Ferns hate being disturbed, so only plant and repot them in late spring/early summer before their summer growth period starts and water them in well. Use a good loam-based compost mixed generously with organic matter such as humus or leaf mould. Keep ferns moist at the roots and in hot weather they will appreciate being misted with water (provided they are out of the sun). Mulch the soil with more organic matter or even gravel to keep the roots cool. Cut dead fronds back in winter to tidy up the plant.

Grasses
Perennials

Currently very fashionable, grasses epitomise the informal look in gardening with their arching leaves and feathery flower heads. Pampas grass has been around for a long time, but it is not suitable for pot culture — much too vigorous. Instead some of the smaller grasses make wonderful container plants. Their variety is perhaps surprising — striped and stippled, short and tall, green, brown, yellow, gold and black, large heads/small heads — an arresting arrangement can be made with grasses alone by combining their various colours and shapes.

Give grasses a loam based compost and water in well to establish their roots, then they can be more or less left to it. Split plants in late spring when the clumps get too big, and feed with liquid fertilizer every three weeks during the growing season. Even the dead leaves look attractive in winter, but cut them off in spring before the new growth starts.

Helychrysum petiolare
Evergreen shrub

One of the staples of container gardening, the relatively unexciting helichrysum is nevertheless a reliable performer and will trail attractively and fill in gaps usefully. The most common form has silver-grey velvety leaves, although there is also a variegated and a yellow leafed variety. It's only real problem is that the stems can become a bit leggy, but this is easily cured by clipping back excessive growth.

Holly/Ilex

Evergreen tree

Happily amenable to cutting and pruning, holly is actually a surprisingly slow growing plant. For container culture it is often cut into shapes like a lollipop on a stick and as such it contributes a formal tone to a patio or entrance way. One of holly's great merits is that it will withstand the wind and as such can be usefully employed as a windbreak. If you want berries on your holly you have to have a female plant and there needs to be a male not too far away, unfortunately there is no way of telling which sex an immature plant belongs to.

Hollies are evergreen and there are many variegated varieties with yellow, white, bright green or gold splashed leaves. Leaf shape can also vary considerable from elongated to round and very prickly to almost prickleless. Berries are traditionally scarlet, but can also be yellow or more rarely, white.

Plant into a large container in autumn or spring (when the weather is mild and moist) into a loam based compost such as John Innes No 3 and provide a stake if necessary. Keep the plant well watered until it is established and continue to water well in dry spells. Any necessary pruning should be done in mid to late summer.

Hosta

Herbaceous perennial

Hostas were the fashionable plant of the 1980s to such an extent that many new varieties were hybridized. Consequently there are many named varieties which differ in leaf size, texture and colouration — various shades of green, cream and yellow. Hostas are not generally grown for their short-lived mid to late summer white or pale blue-violet flowers which appear on spikes above the foliage.

Hostas like to be grown out of the sun in a damp and shady location in moist loam based compost. Hostas form clumps, the larger ones grow to a height and spread of around 3ft (90cm) — though a few varieties are much bigger. Only split mature plants after about four years when they fill their container, but mulch and water them well throughout the growing season. Hostas die back completely in late autumn and only start to push shoots through the soil in spring when the weather warms up. Unfortunately they are absolute magnets for slugs and snails.

Ivy/*Hedera helix*

Perennial evergreen climber

Where would a container gardener be without ivy? This indispensable plant will fill any vertical or horizontal gap in sun or shade and it doesn't even need tying in — it clings all by itself by means of aerial roots! There are many named varieties which offer different leaf shapes and sizes as well as variation in colour, from dark to bright green, and yellow, grey and white variegation. The tiny white flowers are insignificant and only appear on mature plants, they later turn into glossy black poisonous berries.

Grow ivy in any type of container in either multi-purpose or loam based compost; keep the compost moist and feed with liquid fertilizer once a month throughout the growing season. If necessary trim straggling shoots back to shape in autumn.

Banana/Musa

Tender tree

Not at all hardy and needing winter protection, the banana is nevertheless great fun to grow and really does give an air of the Tropics. Some species are

Above: Variegated plants come into their own in the darker months of winter and early spring when the brightness of their leaves makes up for the lack of flowers elsewhere. Here a lollipop clipped holly is joined temporarily by white cyclamen.

Right: *Euphorbia characias* ssp *wulfenii* in common with all spurges, looks dramatic, but contains a poisonous sap.

INFORMATIVE & INSPIRATIONAL IDEAS FOR CONTAINER GARDENING

---

provides the perfect foil for other more extravagant plants. Happy to grow in any reasonable well-drained soil, in sun or partial shade privet is an adaptable plant which can be clipped to form a neat shape; the variegated varieties such as 'Aureum' require full sunshine to thrive.

For a roof garden privet makes a useful windbreak as well as privacy provider. Privet will grow quite large — up to 6ft (2m) or more high so give it a large container. Clip young plants back hard for the first two years to produce good, strong, dense growth, after which just clip to shape as required.

Saxifrage
Perennial
A large family of low-growing rosette-forming plants some evergreen some not. Many are grown as alpines and thus require semi-sun and free-draining compost. The species vary considerably in their requirements and should be treated according to their label.

Senecio
Various
A huge family of widely varied plants, most senecios suitable for container growing are low-growing succulents useful for a trough or windowbox. One exception is the deeply cut, silvery-white, velvet leaved *Senecio cineraria* (also sometimes called *S.maritima*) a very popular and

widely-grown foliage plant which provides a striking contrast with many different flowers and colour schemes. 'Silver Dust' is the most reliable form.

Although strictly speaking a perennial, it is mostly grown as an annual as older growth can get rather straggly and woody. This variety produces yellow flowers but they are best removed as they rather detract from the beauty of the plant.

Vine/Vitis
Deciduous perennial climber
Hardly needing any introduction, the grapevine is redolent of the Mediterranean lifestyle where they are grown to provide shelter from the sun. Vines are vigorous, greedy plants so grow them in a large container filled with humus-rich, John Innes No3 and water and feed regularly throughout the growing season. Given sufficient room, a vine can grow 20ft (6m) or more. Grow in the sunniest spot possible and provide heavyweight support such as a wall or secure trellis for it to grow up.

Viticulture is an art form in itself, but in a good summer even an ordinary vine will produce attractive bunches of grapes (though these are not always edible). However, the vine has to be female to produce grapes and needs a male within pollination distance. Unfortunately there is no way of knowing whether an unspecified plant will be male or female — only time will tell.

Yew/Taxus
Evergreen tree
Although a large tree the yew is slow enough growing to be amenable to container culture in early life (they can last over a thousand years!) When clipped to shape yew makes an attractive formal plant and is a useful foil to other more exuberant performers. The needle-like leaves are usually dark green, but golden forms such as 'Aurea' are widely available. Grow yew in good rich compost and feed and water regularly in the growing season.

Yucca
Evergreen perennial
The stiff sword-like leaves which grow out of a central clump of the yucca add a formal, architectural element to a container garden as well as a touch of the exotic. Despite this they are very hardy provided they have well drained soil and do not have wet roots in winter.

Given plenty of sunshine and not too much water the yucca will grow to a good 6ft (2m) high and wide and produce a massive flowering stem of large creamy-white, lily-like flowers in summer. Cut these off after flowering.

Herbs

Bay/*Laurus nobilis*
Evergreen tree
Somewhat tender when grown in
containers the bay tree needs to be
protected from cold winter winds
which damage young growth. It enjoys
a position in the full sun in a well
drained large container with a rich
compost such as John Innes No 3. In a
large container it can grow to 8–10ft
(2.4–3m) high.

Bay makes a good topiary plant as
it can be clipped to shape without
danger of damaging the plant. Its dark
green, leathery leaves are used in sauces
for its distinctive flavouring. The bay
flowers in late spring with clusters of
unexciting yellow flowers.

Chives/*Allium schoenoprasum*
Perennial bulb
These small members of the onion
family grow very easily into quite large
clumps in containers whether in sun or
partial shade. Their hollow green stems
are used in salads and reach between
4–24in (10–60cm) high. Soft purple-
pink flowers appear during the
summer, after which their stems
toughen up slightly, but they can still
be used in cooking and salads.

Coriander/*Coriandrum sativum*
Annual
Increasingly popular in mixed salads
and exotic dishes, the leaves of
coriander have an invigoratingly fresh
aroma. Grow the plant in a good
sunny position in a rich but well-

drained compost. Harvest the leaves
young before they toughen up. Do not
allow the plant to flower unless you
want to collect the seeds as this signals
the end of its life. Like fennel and dill
it is a member of the *Umbelliferae*
family so it bears its tiny white flowers
in large flat heads.

Dill/*Anethum graveolens*
Hardy annual, biannual herb
Both the leaves and seeds of the dill
plant are used in cooking, especially in
association with fish. It grow to around
3ft (90cm) tall with large flat heads of
tiny yellow flowers and fine, filigree
leaves growing from one upright
hollow stem. The flowers are followed
by seeds in late summer. Dill requires
well drained soil and a sunny position

Fennel/*Foeniculum vulgare*
Annual and perennial
Fennel seeds have a strong aniseed
flavour and the leaves somewhat less
so. It is a very similar plant to dill and

Top: Marjoram is a useful
herb to grow for its looks —
especially in variegated form
as with *Origanum vulgare*
'Gold Tip' and for eating.

Above: Parsley is perhaps
the most commonly used
herb of all. However it is a
handsome plant in its own
right and deserves to be
grown for its foliage alone.

INFORMATIVE &
INSPIRATIONAL
IDEAS FOR
CONTAINER
GARDENING

is also used in fish dishes and salads. It enjoys well drained soil in the full sun but must be kept well watered to prevent the plant bolting and going to seed. Its tall hollow stems grow to 6ft (2m) high with frothy fine foliage and large flat heads of minute yellow flowers. Grow it well away from dill as the plants readily cross-pollinate and produce intermediate tasting seeds.

Lemon balm/*Melissa officianalis*
Perennial
A vigorous plant best grown on its own or alongside other equally robust plants. The leaves have a delicious lemon scent and for this reason can be put into cold summer drinks and teas. Lemon balm grows to 2ft (0.6m) tall but dies back to the ground each winter. Variegated varieties have splashes of golden yellow on the leaves. It likes a moist soil and can cope with partial shade. The flowers are insignificant so the plant is best cut back regularly to encourage bushiness.

Lemon verbena/*Aloysia triphylla*
Perennial small shrub
For sheer delightful lemony fragrance nothing beats the lemon verbena (also still found as *Lippia citriodora*). Unfortunately it is not reliably hardy except in the most sheltered positions so it requires winter protection. Coming all the way from South America, lemon verbena enjoys as much sunshine as it can get and a light, well drained soil. Bushes can

grow up to 4ft (1.2m) tall but will die back somewhat in winter. Grow it near a pathway where you'll get a waft of its fragrance as you brush past. The whiteish-purple flowers appear throughout the summer in clusters on the tips of the stem which while small, are nevertheless attractive. Clip off the flower trusses as they finish to encourage more leaves.

Marjoram/Oraganum
Hardy perennial
Another large aromatic family valuable for their cooking properties. Different varieties have variegated or coloured leaves or bracts. Marjoram requires a sunny position in well drained soil where it receives good air circulation; in cold weather marjoram hates to sit in damp soil and will die as a consequence. Pinch out the growing tips for a bushier plant, although this will delay production of its small but attractive (to people and insects) heads of pink, purple or white flowers.

Parsley/*Petroselinum crispum*
Hardy biennial
Valued as an ornamental plant as well as a herb, parsley is claimed to be the most widely grown herb in Europe. Used as a garnish in cooking it grows as two distinct types — curly (preferred in Britain) and flat (grown on the Continent). The former for strictly cultivation reasons is better for container growing as it remains shorter, about 12in (30cm), and

neater. Parsley needs a rich, well drained soil and plenty of sunshine. Crop the plant regularly once mature to stop it getting leggy and to prevent the production of its flat heads of flowers (umbels).

Mint/Mentha
Hardy perennial
There are many different varieties of mint each with varying types of menthol aroma — lemon, ginger and pineapple — as well as degrees of mintiness. Most of them are extremely vigorous plants which will readily overwhelm their neighbours, and everything from ground-hugging to 3 or 4ft (90–1.2m) high. They are best grown alone in their own container. All have purplish-pink flowers in the summer to which bees and other insects are attracted. Mint is easily grown in sun or partial shade and is not fussy about the type of soil in which it grows, however it must be moist for the plant to thrive.

Rosemary/Rosmarinus
Evergreen perennial shrub
No garden — container or otherwise — is complete without rosemary's spicy, peppery aroma. Grow it near a pathway where it can be brushed against frequently. A neat and attractive spring flowering bush rosemary can be clipped to shape to form a neat mound, or left to its own devices. Some varieties are stiffly upright ('Miss Jessopp's Upright'),

others arch ('Benenden Blue') while the prostratus group creep along the ground. The needle-like leaves are usually dark green and the flowers almost always degrees of blue, although there are pinks and whites.

Sage/Salvia
Biennial/perennial
A huge plant family containing many and varied plants. Common sage (*Salvia officinalis*) is the most widely grown and is available in different varieties with variegated, tri-coloured (green, cream and purple) and purple leaves. Mature plants grow up to 32in (80cm) with an even wider spread, although 'Tricolor' is somewhat less vigorous and more suited to pot culture. In summer tall flower spikes appear with blue, mauve, white, pink

Below: Rosemary, green sage, thyme and marjoram are growing happily together, showing that even a small windowbox will yield a respectable crop of fresh herbs.

Right: What could be nicer! This collection of basils needs plenty of sunshine and water to thrive. The plants also require regular pinching out to keep the plants bushy as they are apt to become leggy.

or purple flowers which are a haven for insects. Grow sage in ordinary, well drained but moist soil in a sunny position.

Sweet Basil/*Ocimum basilicum*
Tender annual/perennial
There are many different types of basil, but the commonest is sweet basil so integral to Italian cooking. Easy to grow provided it gets plenty of sunshine and water, it is though a magnet for trouble — aphids especially whitefly, red spider, snails and slugs. To prevent such damage, grow basil in rich moist compost, high off the ground where fresh air can circulate, and mist the leaves over frequently (though not while the sun is on it). The plant loses its vigour after flowering, so regularly pinch out the growing tips to both encourage bushiness and prevent flowering.

Tarragon/*Artemisia dracunculus*
Perennial herb
Also known as French tarragon this plant makes an attractive small bushy shrub about 3ft (1m) high. Do not on any account confuse it with Russian tarragon (*A. dracunculoides*) which is a much tougher, bitter and more vigorous plant. Tarragon is not completely hardy and will only survive the winter in a very sheltered position. In common with all herbs it likes a sunny situation with free-draining soil. Its slim green leaves are used in salads, sauces and vinegar.

Thyme/Thymus
Hardy perennial, small shrub
The familiar and unmistakable aroma of thyme has long been a garden favourite as well as a kitchen essential. There are many different varieties to choose from all with varying qualities and growth habits. Most thymes are low-growing and some even ground-hugging, but they all require very well drained soil and plenty of sunshine. Thyme will die in cold weather if its roots remain wet. *Thymus vulgaris* — common thyme — is the type most often grown, it has small dark green leaves which in some varieties ('Silver Posie') are silver coloured, variegated or lighter green. In summer pinkish-purple flower heads appear above the foliage attracting nectar-loving insects. Clip off the dead heads after flowering to encourage new growth and bushiness.

Wormwood/*Artemisia absinthium*
Hardy perennial
A member of the large artemisia family which are grown for the beauty of their light-reflecting grey-green filigree leaves. One of the commonest is wormwood, a really bitter herb, which grows to about 3ft (1m) tall. It can be clipped to form a neat hump. Grow artemisia in full sun in light well drained soil and cut back straggling shoots as necessary. However grow it on its own well away from your culinary herbs because it contains a growth-inhibiting toxin which will adversely affect nearby plants .

KEEPING YOUR PLANTS HEALTHY

Here we come to the biggest disadvantage of growing plants in containers — they need constant vigilance. Not that they are hard to look after, but they do need regular care to flourish.

Right: Pinching back with your fingers or secateurs will encourage the growth of new shoots and reduce the length of straggling stems. In addition, lightly pruning your plants in this way is not only good for them, it can also be greatly therapeutic for you.

THE main requirement of container grown plants — especially in hot weather — is regular watering: this can mean two or three times a day for plants in exposed situations such as hanging baskets and in full sun. Otherwise a good soaking once a day in the morning before the sun lies on them, or in the early evening after the strength of the sun has disappeared. Never water plants in the sun unless absolutely necessary, as drops of water on the leaves and petals will act like mini magnifying glasses and scorch and disfigure the plant.

Establish a regular feeding routine if you didn't use a control release fertilizer at planting time. The frequency of use depends on the type you use, the packet will give the regularity and dosage.

Plants in containers are artificially stimulated to grow and flower, consequently they need constant picking over for the removal of dead flower heads and dropping leaves. Regular dead-heading of plants such as petunias will encourage the growth of more flowers. This is because annuals (plants whose life-cycle lasts a year) need to produce seed for the next season, if the plant is frustrated in this by having the unformed seed capsule (the dead head) removed, it will then produce more buds in the hope of producing seed. This is true of many plants, but especially of annuals.

This tidying up of plants is one of the great therapeutic aspects of gardening, and most gardeners do

INFORMATIVE &
INSPIRATIONAL
IDEAS FOR
CONTAINER
GARDENING

Training Climbers

One of the most effective ways of making the most
of container grown plants is to grow some of the
plants upwards to add a vertical dimension to your
display. Many plants are natural climbers anyway
and only require some support to grow up. Others
only manage to grow upwards — as opposed to
sprawling along the ground — by being tied into
supports. Such help for climbing plants can be as
simple as a wall with some wires or trellis work
attached or ordinary garden canes, ornamental
obelisks, archways and wire frames of various sorts
and shapes.

Climbers by nature tend to be more vigorous
plants than most, so will need tying in to their
supports every couple of weeks throughout the
growing season. They will also need trimming back
to shape to contain their exuberance. As a rule of
thumb, prune plants to shape immediately after
flowering — unless they go on to produce
interesting or useful fruits — that way you are less
likely to lose the next flush of flowers. As with all
pruning, always cut the growth back to just above
a healthy-looking bud with a clean diagonal cut.
The bud will then take over from the previous
shoot and grow away in another direction. In some
plants this cutting back will encourage more than
one bud to 'break' which in time makes the plant
considerably bushier.

**Right: Staking a climber to a trellis. Insert the trellis frame
into the plant pot before putting in the plant. Then, having
planted your climber, carefully remove any existing supports
(such as a cane). Carefully untangle the twisted stems and
arrange them to spread evenly across the trellis. Using
either plastic ties or twine, very gently tie the plant to the
trellis in as many places as the plant needs support. When
the job is complete — take the time to do it properly — the
result should provide a perfect framework for the plant.**

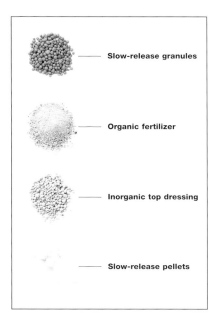

Slow-release granules

Organic fertilizer

Inorganic top dressing

Slow-release pellets

it in a casual way anyway as they
look over their plants. This is also
an opportunity to carry out a little
light pruning. By pinching back —
literally with your fingers or
secateurs — you can reduce the
length of any straggling stems; do
this to just in front of a bud or
healthy branch. This encourages
the plant to 'break' and grow two
or three new shoots where only one
grew before.

Pests and Diseases

Above: The larvae of butterflies and moths, caterpillars have long tubular bodies and vary greatly in colour and size. The one constant is their voracious appetite leading to the damage or defoliation of plants.

INFORMATIVE & INSPIRATIONAL **IDEAS** FOR CONTAINER GARDENING

As with garden plants those grown in containers are prone to pests and disease. A whole host of problems are possible and many plants have their own individual weaknesses, but, generally speaking, only a few common problems are likely to be encountered. Prevention is by far the best cure, so keep your plants healthy and well watered — a sickly, neglected plant is much more susceptible to problems. Check your plants regularly, especially the young growth and buds and the under sides of leaves. Many potential disasters can be averted by early recognition and rapid action. For example, greenfly can be simply rubbed off with the fingers and slugs, snails and caterpillars can be removed by hand. There are various ways to treat pests and diseases once they have arisen, it depends on the seriousness of the problem and whether you want to use an organic method, which means using no chemicals at all — man made or naturally occurring. Organic methods concentrate on the quality of the soil and work upwards, they also tolerate and allow for a small degree of damage. Essentially organic gardeners believe that with less chemical interference nature will control and restore a natural balance.

Organic methods include hand picking and removal of pests, the use of natural predators to either eat or parasatize pests, and the use of soapy water or methylated spirits to remove pests. To discover the range of organic controls look for specialist organic suppliers advertising in gardening magazines, most of them have mail order catalogues.

Chemicals are the first resort of many gardeners, they must be used sparingly and selectively if they are not to have a wider effect than intended — many beneficial insects and animals can die as a result of unconsidered usage. Before buying chemicals read the packaging carefully to discover exactly what the contents will control, some are formulated to be highly selective in the pests they will effect — but also which plants they will damage. Also look to see how long the chemical will persist once it has been applied; the most toxic chemicals are nolonger legally available, but many readily available concoctions are still poisonous.

Pesticides — to control pests, and fungicides — to control diseases, can both be applied in spray form. This involves mixing a proportion of formula with a larger proportion of water. Some come ready mixed in a sprayer or aerosol. Never use the same sprayer for any other purpose as lurking chemical residues could cause considerable damage.

Other methods of application include dusts which are puffed onto the trouble spots, and smokes which release chemical into the atmosphere, but these can only be used in a confined space such as a glasshouse.

Spraying works in one of three

ways: firstly by anticipating possible problems and acting to prevent their occurrence; secondly by spraying with a contact chemical when the problem occurs; or thirdly by using a systemic insecticide. With this latter approach the plant absorbs the chemical and when the sap-sucking predator feeds on the plant it is poisoned; this is especially useful if the insect pest has rolled itself up into the leaves where a contact spray cannot reach it. Be very careful with chemical sprays if you are planning on eating the plant in question — read the instructions for use very carefully before buying — and beware of spray drift, chemicals can stray onto nearby plants in even the lightest breeze.

Below is a quick run through of the most common problems the container gardener is most likely to encounter.

Aphids

There are many different types of aphid which vary in colour from white through to black in almost every colour except blue, however the one most likely to be encountered by the container gardener — indeed any gardener — is the greenfly. These are are small bright green, fleshy flying insects which in the initial stages of infestation are found on the undersides of young leaves and on fresh young shoots and buds. They feed by sucking the sap out of plants, thus weakening and distorting new growth. After eating — which they do continuously —

aphids excrete excess sugars and water in sticky drops known as honeydew. This leaves the plant and often its surrounds too, sticky and attractive particularly to ants, it also encourages the growth of black sooty mould.

In warm weather aphids can mature within a week and multiply at an astonishing rate, and if left unchecked will within a short time cover all the new growth on a plant, as well as spread to nearby plants. Aphids also carry viruses from diseased plants to healthy plants — which can spread a problem.

The greenfly's more unsightly relative is the blackfly, a common invader on nasturtiums in particular.

The most effective control of aphids is by spraying and there are many different types of chemical available for this. Organic spraying with a soap solution — a good quality washing-up liquid is best for this — will only be a partial control and other measures, such as hand removal will also be necessary.

Caterpillars

In layman's terms caterpillars are not much more than eating machines — they can devastate a plant within a few hours reducing leaves to lacy stumps and devouring new shoots and buds. Caterpillar attacks can be overnight and terminal — but this is extreme, most can be stopped by simple hand removal before too much damage has been done, but

this does rely on regular inspection of the plants.

Caterpillars are the larval stage between egg and either butterfly or moth, so not all are to be discouraged as some become beautiful and increasingly rare insects. However most caterpillars will be only pest species such a cabbage whites and nondescript grey moths.

Some caterpillars roll themselves up in terminal leaf buds or young leaves within which they spin their cocoon. In this case careful hand removal of the encased caterpillar is the only possible way to rescue the shoots, but very often this is too late as the pupae will already have eaten.

To control caterpillars check the undersides of leaves for eggs and crush them off with your fingers or remove the caterpillars by hand — though if in doubt about them wear protective gloves as some of the species, especially the hairy ones, can contain skin irritants. Chemical sprays which work on contact can be used against caterpillars if the infestation is bad; systemic pesticides are less successful with caterpillars than with aphids.

Cats and dogs

Pets in the garden can be a real nuisance: they will deter the wildlife you do want — birds, frogs, toads, butterflies — and ignore the troublemakers you don't want — snails, slugs, aphids etc. Dogs and cats generally don't tamper with the plants

Above: Though unlikely to cause major harm to plants and pots, cats and dogs can be a nuisance in the garden. Whilst deterrents are available, unlike most other pests, there is no sure-fire way of protecting your garden from the damage caused by our furry friends.

INFORMATIVE &
INSPIRATIONAL
IDEAS FOR
CONTAINER
GARDENING

themselves — the notable exception being catmint (nepeta) which felines seem unable to resist eating and also rolling on. Dogs can be a problem with their exuberance (especially wagging tails) knocking over plants and thrashing through bushes, but at least the animal is likely to be your own, unlike cats for whom a garden fence is no boundary.

There are a number of proprietary deterrents which claim to keep animals at bay: reports differ widely as to their effectiveness.

Moulds and Mildews
Grey mould occurs when a fleshy leaved or stemmed plant starts to rot and a grey fungal growth appears on the damaged tissue, often starting at the crown of the plant. There are many different kinds of mould, most of which come from infection by air-borne spores. The trouble can spread rapidly so quick action is necessary. In the first instance remove the offending plant material and burn it or otherwise destroy it; then use a systemic fungicide to eliminate it. If the entire plant is very badly affected the only answer may be to destroy the plant completely.

Powdery mildew is a fungal disease which attacks the young soft and fleshy leaves of plants such as begonia. A specially formulated fungal spray will deal with the problem.

Red Spider Mite
These minute pests thrive in dry conditions so are most commonly found in glasshouses but will occasionally occur during hot weather on plants in sheltered positions outside between June and September. Usually the first sign of their arrival is a yellow mottling of the leaves and a fine webbing between the stems caused by the insects sucking the sap and cell contents from the plant tissue. If left untreated the leaves and shoots will turn brown and desiccated.

Females hibernate over winter re-emerging in spring in the warmer weather to lay their eggs and start the cycle again. So a good degree of control can be instigated with a thorough cleaning and disposal of all loose plant litter and dry leaves. The best method of control is by misting the affected plants with ordinary water a couple of times a day — the mites dislike moisture and humidity.

Slugs and Snails
These are the bane of many a gardener's life as they can destroy an entire plant within a few hours. Slugs and snails especially enjoy juicy young growth and fleshy plants such as hostas on which they are notorious. They also like to feed on spring bulbs (daffodils, hyacinths, tulips etc) and can cause such extensive damage from which the plant never recovers. However by growing plants in containers they are kept somewhat at bay, but as these mollusks can climb vertical surfaces they take a lot of keeping out. They especially like

sheltering behind piles of stones, or inside the overhanging rim of a pot, so look for them there. A particularly rewarding time to collect slugs and snails is at dusk on a warm evening after a rain shower — they come out of hiding in their droves to enjoy the moist air. As they are mostly night-time eaters hunting with a torch can be very satisfying for an enraged gardener!

Slug damage is indicated by ragged holes in leaves, stems, roots and flowers, furthermore stems are often partially gnawed through, but the real give-away is the silvery slime trail they leave behind — this can sometimes be followed back to their lair. Be ruthless with slugs and snails, collect and dispose of them when you find them for you will only ever find a small proportion of their real numbers.

Birds such as thrushes enjoy eating slugs and snails, but they are unlikely to dispose of them in sufficient numbers. Organic methods of control other than by hand removal include the use of 'slug pubs' — these are simply bowls or small jars sunk into the ground and filled with beer (or cider). The mollusk is attracted by the smell, falls into the drink and drowns happy. The beer is good for two or three nights before changing.

Alternatively use inverted grapefruit skins, cabbage leaves or sacking laid on the ground. The slugs will hide underneath during the day. Gravel and sharp stone chippings scattered around the plants discourage slugs as well.

Non-organic methods include chemical soil drenches and slug pellets, both of which are effective for two or three days. Care needs to be taken though with their use near pets and small children — follow the safety instructions on the package carefully.

Vine Weevils

This is becoming an increasingly common pest which is being spread in the compost of pot plants and container grown plants — even unwittingly by some reputable nurseries. To all intents this pest is invisible until its damage is conclusive. Vine weevils eat away the root systems of plants, which then collapse completely and are usually beyond rescue before the problem can be stopped. When knocking plants out of their containers before potting on, check for small white grubs up to 0.3in (8mm) long within the soil. These are the vine weevil larvae which do all the damage as they eat to grow into adults. While still in the soil the somewhat bigger adults take on the form of a translucent, whitish beetle. Immediately destroy grubs and adults and check the rest of the soil, especially around the roots, for more.

The mature vine weevil is a small slow moving dark brown, generally nocturnal, beetle-like creature with a hard carapace. It emerges from the soil throughout the warm months, climbs up the plant and goes looking for more soil in which to lay its eggs. Destroy

any of these you find too. The adults don't in themselves do much damage beyond making a few holes in leaves, but their larval stage is devastating.

Vine weevil are hard to control effectively once they get into your plant collection. A new preparation has recently become available to the amateur gardener called Bio Provado Vine Weevil Killer. This is claimed to be very effective but it should not be used indiscriminately for fear of the weevils developing immunity to the chemical. Organically, other than collecting grubs and beetles by hand, the only solution is to introduce a parasite which feeds on and kills the weevil.

Whitefly

These minute white flying insects are most commonly found on plants growing under glass but can also infest some outdoor plants. They cluster on the undersides of leaves and can increase rapidly in numbers. Like aphids they leave sticky honeydew which in turn encourages sooty mould. Whitefly feed on plant sap which reduces the plant's vigour and leads to yellow spotting on the leaves. Each insect lives for around 7–8 weeks and will breed year-round in warm conditions, but only in the summer outdoors.

Treatment for whitefly on outdoor plants is by chemical spray as fumigants are only suitable for glasshouses. Organically a parasite called *Encarsia formosa* is very effective, but again only for a glasshouse.

Index